The Routes of English

3 by Simon Elmes

Published by BBC Adult Learning
201 Wood Lane,
London W12 7TS

Commissioning Editor: Angie Mason
Editor: Anne Barnes, Julie Delf
Design: Anne McCarry
CD Replication: Forward Sound and Vision
Printing: Geoff Neal Litho Ltd

ISBN: 1 9017 1024 6

FOREWORD BY MELVYN BRAGG

The Routes of English go marching on. Now down great highways, now down small byways, now opening up little paths that have been closed for centuries.

Routes 1 was a general historical survey of how spoken English evolved from its origins in local speech to a national tongue.

Routes 2 looked at five themes which contributed to and have been shaped by the evolution of 1000 years of speaking the language.

In this book we look at the languages which did not evolve into a national standard. This could be called location English. It is English spoken and exercised by people who themselves, until very recently, might never have travelled more than a mile or two away from where they were born. The idea is that by looking at the local dialects now and by attempting to examine the way in which these local landscape languages have developed, we are looking at a different story – one of sudden change.

It is inevitably the story of closed communities – pit men in Northumbria, for instance, china clay workers and fishermen in Cornwall. These have both a sadness and a reverberation of vitality which make their study fascinating.

As ever, we are looking again at how change is affecting language. We who make the programmes, like those who have listened, are intrigued by – and have been immersed in – the spread from small beginnings of what has become a world language and a world of dialects.

INTRODUCTION BY SIMON ELMES

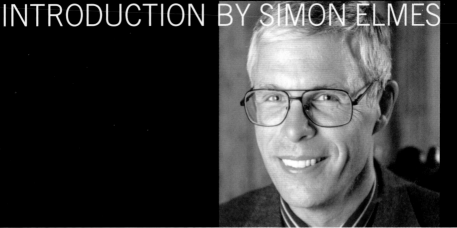

Growing up in Bristol in the 1950s made me aware of just how rich local talk could be. The fact that the very name Bristol allegedly arose from the local habit of attaching an 'l' sound to hanging vowels, especially 'o's and 'a's, at the end of words, caught my imagination. So medieval 'Bristowe' gained a final 'l' and was transformed into 'Bristol'. It amazed me that this linguistic peculiarity, which I heard literally every day around me, should stretch back in time to when places were being named.

It is also the basis of the popular Bristol joke about the man complaining of bad TV reception in the city. He is told by the engineer that the problem came from his aerial. 'I know that', comes the reply, 'that's what I want you to fix!'. 'No,' rejoins the engineer, 'not the aerial on your roof. The areal where you live!' The idea that Elizabethan Bristolians – or even earlier – had been prone to change 'opera' into 'operal' and 'Maria' into 'Marial' delighted me.

So when I met a man called Stanley Ellis in the early 1980s, I was agog to hear more about the vastly different and complicated ways regional Britain spoke to itself. Stanley was – is – the guru of dialect in Britain (though 'dialect' is a term he rejects as too imprecise, preferring 'local speech' or 'local talk'). I also knew he had a reputation as a bit of a Professor Higgins, able to identify a speaker's origins by the sounds he or she made. So we plotted a series of programmes on dialect for Radio 4, to be called *Talk of the Town, Talk of the Country*. It eventually ran to eighteen separate investigations of local speech, literally from Land's End to the Western Isles, and was broadcast in the early 1980s. When Melvyn Bragg and I were discussing the shape of *The Routes of*

English, we felt that it was probably high time that BBC Radio 4 had another listen to how local talk was faring in Britain. Twenty years ago, what had struck Stanley Ellis and me almost everywhere we went was that the eternal lament 'dialect is dying', was, for the most part, completely untrue. From the pitmen of Northumberland to the denizens of Troubled Belfast to the fishermen of Lowestoft, we found huge variety and vigour in the vocabulary, syntax and accent of local speakers. It was changing, evolving, just as, for instance, farming methods moved towards agribusiness and away from the 'horse-hoeing husbandry' that had been the norm until the Second World War. But dying? No way. The dozens of school-age children we got talking to proved that conclusively.

Only in the Thames Valley was there a difference. There the influx of new companies and industries and the people to staff them had long changed the principal activity from agriculture to industry, from farm to pharmaceuticals. There we really felt that the old Berkshire dialect of Claud Corderoy (a farm-worker-turned-bricklayer) and his friends was a lost cause, a threatened species. So what would the verdict be at the start of the twenty-first century?

In Wigton, in Cumbria, which figures in the first *Routes of English* book, we met a bunch of sixth-formers who were very proud of their local talk: 'straw' was *stree* and they all were conversant with and even sometimes used a *gripe* – a three-pronged fork. So we knew it would not all be bad news. But this time we deliberately chose to investigate places where social change was quite likely to have had an impact on the way people spoke.

For this series, Melvyn Bragg's first port of call is Ashington in Northumberland. There pit closures have forced change on the community and necessarily driven out the old language of the pit. What are the youngsters of Ashington talking about – and how – in the year 2000? Derry has seen some of the worst conflicts of the quarter-century of Ulster Troubles, so has the arrival of relative stability made an impression on local talk? In deepest Cornwall, the tin mines have now all closed for good, the English China Clay company is French-owned, agriculture is in decline and a vast percentage of the inhabitants are now incomers. Can Cornish dialect – and the glimmering revival of the old Cornish language survive? With the success of comedian Ali G on television, we know that a form of (albeit pseudo-) inner-city black talk has gained a level of popularity and familiarity nationwide. So what is being spoken on the streets of Brixton in London right now? And where does it originate? Finally, we look at what happens when English rubs shoulders for a thousand years with another proud British linguistic tradition, the Welsh language. To find out, we have travelled to the little market town of Oswestry, five miles into England, but once part of Wales...

Wherever we went, we found riches. But since dialect is essentially a spoken idiom, rendering it on the page has presented a challenge. We hope you will feel that we have made the examples we use as clear and as 'audible' as possible. For the real experience, of course, you must read the text in conjunction with the truly audible riches of the accompanying CDs. And, above all, we hope you will enjoy this latest journey along *The Routes of English.*

contents

1

TRACKING THE TALK

The International Phonetic
Alphabet first published in
1889, this was the first
scientific system to devise
signs that would describe
the sounds of European
and other languages.

There's a joke told in Belfast about the wee boy who cries out that his mate has fallen in the river. When the river is scoured but no person alive or dead recovered, the boy protests that he'd never said anybody had fallen in the river. 'It's mi mate,' he replies, 'the mate (meat) outta mi sandwich!'

The point of the story in the context of *The Routes of English* is that it highlights two interesting features that we are going to be considering time and again throughout this book. First is that the joke only works where the two words *meat* and *mate* are pronounced identically, are precise homophones. This means that it is distinctly a local joke, a joke built round a collision of sound and meaning that doesn't occur in standard English and that you will only find in Ulster and a few other parts of the country.

The other feature that the little tale highlights is the spoken quality of dialectal English. Regional talk is just that – talk. Write it down and you are immediately in problems. This is both one of the glories and one of the intrinsic difficulties that any student of regional English has to contend with. How to record the talk for posterity?

Until the invention of the International Phonetic Alphabet in the late nineteenth century – which provided a formula for recording the relationships between lips, tongue, palate, teeth and dental ridge, not to mention the uvula – local talk had to rely on the 26 letters of the standard English alphabet for rendering words on the page.

And very inadequate they were. Indeed, open many a dialect dictionary or look up one of the many fine pieces of prose or poetry written in regional English today and you will find strange blends of vowel and consonant that work overtime to transcribe

THE INTERNATIONAL PHONETIC ALPHABET (revised to 1993)

CONSONANTS (PULMONIC)

	Bilabial	Labiodental	Dental	Alveolar	Postalveolar	Retroflex	Palatal	Velar	Uvular	Pharyngeal	Glottal
Plosive	p b			t d		ʈ ɖ	c ɟ	k g	q ɢ		ʔ
Nasal	m	ɱ		n		ɳ	ɲ	ŋ	N		
Trill	ʙ			r					R		
Tap or Flap				ɾ		ɽ					
Fricative	ɸ β	f v	θ ð	s z	ʃ ʒ	ʂ ʐ	ç ʝ	x ɣ	χ ʁ	ħ ʕ	h ɦ
Lateral fricative				ɬ ɮ							
Approximant		ʋ		ɹ		ɻ	j	ɰ			
Lateral approximant				l		ɭ	ʎ	L			

Where symbols appear in pairs, the one to the right represents a voiced consonant. Shaded areas denote articulations judged impossible.

CONSONANTS (NON-PULMONIC)

Clicks	Voiced implosives	Ejectives
ʘ Bilabial	ɓ Bilabial	' as in:
ǀ Dental	ɗ Dental/alveolar	p' Bilabial
ǃ (Post)alveolar	ʄ Palatal	t' Dental/alveolar
ǂ Palatoalveolar	ɠ Velar	k' Velar
ǁ Alveolar lateral	ʛ Uvular	s' Alveolar fricative

VOWELS

Where symbols appear in pairs, the one to the right represents a rounded vowel.

OTHER SYMBOLS

ʍ Voiceless labial-velar fricative   ɕ ʑ Alveolo-palatal fricatives
w Voiced labial-velar approximant   ɺ Alveolar lateral flap
ɥ Voiced labial-palatal approximant   ɧ Simultaneous ʃ and x
ʜ Voiceless epiglottal fricative
ʢ Voiced epiglottal fricative   Affricates and double articulations can be represented by two symbols joined by a tie bar if necessary.
ʡ Epiglottal plosive   k͡p t͡s

SUPRASEGMENTALS

'	Primary stress	foʊnəˈtɪʃən
ˌ	Secondary stress	
ː	Long	eː
ˑ	Half-long	eˑ
˘	Extra-short	ĕ
.	Syllable break	ɹi.ækt
|	Minor (foot) group	
‖	Major (intonation) group	
‿	Linking (absence of a break)	

TONES & WORD ACCENTS

	LEVEL			CONTOUR	
	e̋ or ˥	Extra high	ě or ˎ	Rising
	é ˦	High	ê ˎ	Falling
	ē ˧	Mid	e᷄ ˎ	High rising
	è ˨	Low	e᷅ ˎ	Low rising
	ȅ ˩	Extra low	e᷈ ˎ	Rising-falling
	↓ Downstep		↗ Global rise	etc.
	↑ Upstep		↘ Global fall	

DIACRITICS

Diacritics may be placed above a symbol with a descender, e.g. ŋ̊

̥	Voiceless	n̥ d̥	̤	Breathy voiced	b̤ a̤	̪	Dental t̪ d̪
̬	Voiced	s̬ t̬	̰	Creaky voiced	b̰ a̰	̺	Apical t̺ d̺
ʰ	Aspirated	tʰ dʰ	̼	Linguolabial	t̼ d̼	̻	Laminal t̻ d̻
̹	More rounded	ɔ̹	ʷ	Labialized	tʷ dʷ	̃	Nasalized ẽ
̜	Less rounded	ɔ̜	ʲ	Palatalized	tʲ dʲ	ⁿ	Nasal release dⁿ
̟	Advanced	u̟	ˠ	Velarized	tˠ dˠ	ˡ	Lateral release dˡ
̠	Retracted	i̠	ˤ	Pharyngealized	tˤ dˤ	̚	No audible release d̚
̈	Centralized	ë	̴	Velarized or pharyngealized ɫ			
̽	Mid-centralized	e̽	̝	Raised	e̝ (ɹ̝ = voiced alveolar fricative)		
̩	Syllabic	n̩	̞	Lowered	e̞ (β̞ = voiced bilabial approximant)		
̯	Non-syllabic	e̯	̘	Advanced Tongue Root	e̘		
˞	Rhoticity	ɚ	̙	Retracted Tongue Root	e̙		

---

the highly non-standard nature of the sounds to be found in dialect right round the country.

In Northumberland, where to *dunsh* is to 'hit', what convention has decreed that this set of sounds should be rendered thus, rather than 'dunch'? In Cornwall, how are we to represent the regional word for a 'mole'? It is *want*. No problems there, you might think. Yet as we all know *want* (the verb meaning 'to desire') is actually

tcelſon ſuð uno eodeq; cþr cu eo de corpe egredi.
tra ⁊ una atq; indiſſimilr ſede ppetue beatitu
dinr mererecur recipi.

The Venerable Bede (673 [probably]–735) was born in Wearmouth, now Sunderland. At 7 he was given to the care of the Abbot of the Monastery at Wearmouth and Jarrow to be raised as a monk. Here he learned Latin, Greek and a little Hebrew. As a scholar he was chiefly known for his *Ecclesiastical History of the English People*, a history of England from the Roman occupation to 731. Knowledge of England before the 8th Century rests mainly on Bede's work, on his painstaking efforts to gather documents and oral testimony. Many consider Bede to be the first modern historian because he was careful to separate fact from legend and because he cited his sources.

Among the other 40 works he wrote was the *Life of St. Cuthbert*, a monk, a solitary, and (briefly) a bishop, regarded in his time as a miracle worker. This is one of the illustrations from Bede's *Life of St.Cuthbert*.

pronounced *[w(nt]*, to rhyme with *font*. Cornish *wants* are, however, strictly like pants with a short 'a'. There are few conventions for recording the shapes of regional sounds on the page, and this spoken tongue suffers many of the similar vagaries that pre-Caxton English had to contend with – i.e. there was no standard.

For our Belfast lad trying to make us corpse with his gag about his mate having fallen in the river, the punchline is a fragile thing. It works only when spoken out loud and mainly only when in the company of similarly-speaking locals. Any other context and it gets lost in a tangle of heavy-handed exegesis.

Of course, when only a small percentage of the population could read English and conversely most linguistic transactions were carried out orally, dialect could flourish unimpeded. Add to this the fact that until even as recently as the last three decades of the twentieth century, Britons tended for the most part to remain for much of their lives within a handful of miles of their birthplace. Then transactions were not only oral but largely between locals.

But spoken language is, by definition, ephemeral. Recording media, before the possibility of capturing the actual sounds of dialect on disc or tape, were, as we have seen, not really up to the task. So the student of regional English has to fight his or her way through a fog of guesswork and confusing local transcriptions before being able to hazard any sort of guess as to how local talk either sounded two, three, four or more centuries ago, or how it changed.

It is surprising, maybe, that it was as recently as the 1940s that a concerted and systematic academic attempt was made to map the way English sounded locally. It came, of course, in tandem with advances in recording technology, which allowed fieldworkers to head off deep into the valleys of the Lake District and into the heart of the mining communities of the North East, set up their disc recorders in fishermen's cottages along the Devon coast and in Suffolk to find out what this England actually sounded like. It was a great exploit, whose creator was Harold Orton, Professor of English Language at the University of Leeds, where the study of local Englishes is still centred to this day.

Before we look at the way Orton and others have set out to record the precise flavour of English dialects, we should perhaps try to pin down exactly what we mean by 'dialect'. In this chapter so far, I have used a number of different expressions to render the notion – local English, local talk, regional speech and so on. For most people, though, the usual word is 'dialect'. So what do we actually mean by it? **Dr Clive Upton** is in charge of the *Survey of English Dialects* at Leeds University and he likes to quote an American dialectologist:

The best definition of dialect that I've come across, I think, is from Raven MacDavid who wrote that it was 'a variety of a language, generally mutually intelligible with other varieties of that language, but set off from them by a unique complex of features of pronunciation, grammar, and vocabulary'.

Stanley Ellis was one of Harold Orton's colleagues on the original *Survey* in the 1940s. He led the team at Leeds until the late 1980s and is still one of the most respected authorities on local talk. He prefers not to use the word 'dialect' at all.

Generally when people think about what's called 'dialect', they think about something of the nineteenth century, an old-fashioned thing. And I don't much like the word 'dialect'. Nowadays it seems to me that words like 'regional

speech', or 'local speech', express more fully what was formerly thought of as 'dialect'. And 'local speech' can encompass all the changes and movements that are taking place.

Whatever you call it, it would be wrong to assume that records of dialect forms of English did not exist before Orton and his team of fieldworkers set out on their great task. Much work was begun in Victorian days, or even earlier, says **Stanley Ellis**:

Oh, yes, you can go even further back. I mean it depends what you're taking in as a book about dialect. Alexander Gill, in 1619, was writing in Latin, but his English representations of his Lincolnshire dialect can still be identified – at least they certainly could thirty or forty years ago, when I was working in Lincolnshire – as still alive today. You can go back even further to an English translation in 1388 when they were describing the northern dialects as 'so sharp slitting and frotting'. I think the assumed superiority of the southerner comes out there, just as much as it does from south-easterners today in terms of language. But as far as study and academic work on dialect is concerned, I suppose really the nineteenth century was the first major period. You've got names like Alexander J Ellis, but particularly the great giant Professor WW Skeat who actually founded an English Dialect Society with local committees at that time, which had been helping to bring forth words for the *Central Dialect Dictionary*. But he disbanded it in 1896 when the great *English Dialect Dictionary* that was edited by Professor Joseph Wright was on its way. In fact, the Yorkshire Committee decided not to disband and transformed itself in 1897 into the Yorkshire Dialect Society, which celebrated its centenary a couple of years ago.

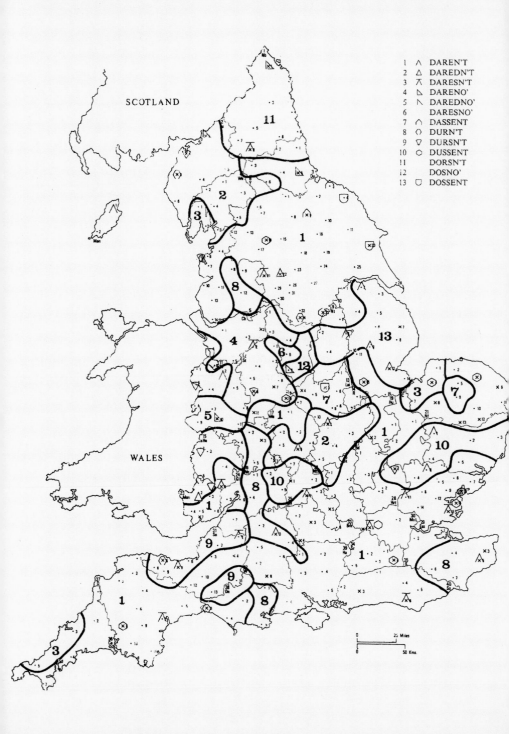

1	∧	DAREN'T
2	△	DAREDN'T
3	⋀	DARESN'T
4	◿	DARENO'
5	⋀	DAREDNO'
6		DARESNO'
7	⌒	DASSENT
8	◇	DURN'T
9	▽	DURSN'T
10	○	DUSSENT
11		DORSN'T
12		DOSNO'
13	⊔	DOSSENT

SCOTLAND

WALES

A map from the *Linguistic Atlas of England*, by Harold Orton illustrating how 'Dare not' was said throughout England in the period 1948–1961. He used a variety of symbols – dots, crosses and other labels – to denote patterns of usage. Orton and his team surveyed 313 rural communities. Speakers tended to be elderly and locally born people with little formal education.

Also from the *Linguistic Atlas of England* this list gives various terms in use to describe a toilet or 'earth-closet'. The term 'shit-house' was actually distributed across 6 areas ranging from Devon to Suffolk and as far north as Yorkshire. From this pattern Orton deduced that the term was actually very widespread in the country.

Earth-closet	house of commons	mizen
bumby-hole	houses of parliament	piss-house
bog	lavatory	out-house
crap-house	lavvy	shit-hole
crapper	littlehouse	thyeveg
earth-lavatory	lobby	vault
garden-house	middy	

Wright's work was a massive step forward in recording the varieties of regional English, but it was a dictionary – a word list rather than an atlas. Its view was essentially retrospective and regarded dialect as something fixed and dead, rather than in a constant state of flux, change and development, with different forms cropping up in differing patterns across the map of the country. With Wright and the various dialect committees, Britain had shown an early lead in the academic study of local talk, but between the wars, we were outpaced by the continentals.

In Germany, for example, they were beginning work on an entirely new idea – that of a 'linguistic atlas', and the *Linguistic Atlas of Germany*, was followed by the *Linguistic Atlas of France*. They'd even done one of the New England states in 1939. So that quite soon, from being ahead of the game, England looked a long way behind. And this was the pressure that was upon people like Harold Orton in the 1930s to get together to make a linguistic atlas of England.

In the slightly arcane world that is the study of English dialects, Harold Orton is a legendary figure. Tough, single-minded and wily, he drove the *Survey of English Dialects* like a train. **Stanley Ellis** made a total of 313 field trips to record local talk:

'Drove' is the right word, because though he was a benevolent man and was a nice man to everybody to knew him, he was absolutely driven by the desire to get his work across. He would work all hours of the day; he wouldn't spare himself, and he wouldn't spare us either.

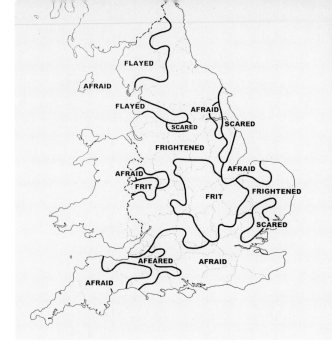

So how did Orton, Stanley Ellis and the rest of the team actually go about plotting the sounds of grassroots English across the country? For five years and through five separate drafts, they worked up a questionnaire containing one hundred standardised questions which were to be put, systematically and without variation, to every interviewee. The subjects were largely selected from farmworkers and rural manual labourers, with as wide a spread of men and women as possible.

The questions were designed, as far as possible, to leave little room for chance mistakes. So where the questionnaire sought to highlight a suspected sound variation, the question was phrased such that only the desired word would be uttered. For example: 'What do you dig the ground with?' was designed to elicit the response 'spade', from which the pronunciation of the vowel in the word and its regional variations could accurately be determined. On the other hand a question like 'What do you call the animal that makes a noise like hee-haw?' was framed to find out which of the many local terms for 'donkey' was most common in a specific area.

Early trial runs of the questionnaire threw up a number of problems, where the required 'default' answer was not forthcoming, and many revisions were made before a finalised standard list was arrived at.

A map from Clive Upton and JDA Widdowson's *Atlas of English Dialects* to show the use of words for 'afraid', a word first introduced by the Normans. 'Frightened' is actually the most widely used word, occurring in all areas even where other words are marked on the map. It derives from the Old English verb 'to fright', although the form 'frightened' was probably first used in the late seventeenth century. The oldest English word for being afraid is 'afeared'.

The Atlas classifies local variations of words for animals, seasons and timings, people, and actions as well as pronunciation and grammar.

The chosen locations for the interviews – reporting stations, they called them – were scattered across the atlas of Britain like grains of pepper, though a casual glance reveals that the distribution is somewhat uneven. Some areas like East Anglia and Cornwall are thinly recorded with only two stations in East Cornwall and barely more than a handful across the whole of that sizeable county. This means that the talk of some areas of England is better described than others, and as we shall see in Chapter 4, the SED threw up only a short list of dialect words in Cornish having their roots in the old Celtic language of the region, whereas modern scholars claim the list runs into the hundreds.

Orton and his team went out into the field armed with their questionnaires and the semi-portable disc recording machines that were, in the early 1950s, the best medium available for field recording. Back in the 1930s, the BBC had sent recording vans into remote corners of Yorkshire and Devon to catch the real sound of how the population of rural England spoke. But where the Leeds team scored was by their scientific rigour and unwavering steadfastness to their task, driven on by the benign tyrant Orton.

So it was that Stanley Ellis would find himself sitting at the kitchen table of an old farmworker, putting him at his ease and then gently firing question after question at him as the swarf of plastic spun off the cutting stylus of the disc-machine. And in so doing, it was recording for the first time ever in any systematic way the true sounds of dialect, as opposed to the inadequate transcriptions of the page that we have already referred to. In fact, to listen to these old recordings, the process was far less formal than the description allows. Laughs were often there in abundance as the old timers told tales to illustrate points that cropped up in the questionnaire. Out of these recordings comes a sense of the deep and relatively unchanging quality of country life, a sound and a ritual that was passed orally down the centuries in these closed communities of like person speaking to like person. **Clive Upton** spoke with pride of the *Survey*:

The *Survey* – or SED, as everybody in the trade calls it – is the only systematic close network survey of the dialects of England that's ever been carried out. So everything that we know about the distribution of forms around the country has to come eventually from the *Survey*. And to that extent it is still very very widely used. That's largely because once that data had been collected from the three hundred and thirteen localities, it was published in its most basic form, and that raw data is there for everyone to use, and it's a great tribute to Harold Orton that it was made completely available to the linguistic community, so it's extremely authoritative. In some respects, of course, certain areas of dialectology have moved away from the immediate direction of the *Survey of English Dialects*, but even in those areas, which it wasn't planned to serve, it's been seen to be extremely useful too.

Drawing on the background of Orton's great work, nearly twenty years ago Stanley Ellis made a broadcast survey of the then current state of local talk in the UK. Across eighteen programmes on BBC Radio 4, called *Talk of the Town, Talk of the Country*, he listened to locals telling stories about their community and their lives, in the most richly accented local talk he and his production team could find. Though the survey was not in any sense scientific, it revealed some interesting half-truths about the supposed decline of local English. In Bristol, the old urban dialect was as rich as ever, but was now being enhanced with Afro-Caribbean terminology from new Bristolians. In Northumberland, the old 'Pitmatic' that was the language of the coalfields was receding slightly and the sound of the Northumbrian uvular 'r' had already become as rare as the boom of the Norfolk bittern. Yet generally speaking, there was no sign of real decline. Only in the Thames Valley, in Berkshire, was the old rural talk now swamped with the rising tide of what has in recent years come to be known as 'Estuary English', the ubiquitous talk of the South-East of England and the media.

The story today is more patchy. But in the current book, we have set out to take a wide perspective on the state of local talk around Britain, seeking not to lament a passing, but rather to celebrate an evolution. For evolution there certainly has been, even in the eighteen or so years since the last BBC enquiry, and certainly in the half-century since Orton was out on the road. New talk is rising to replace the old, and as horizons and expectations broaden, language needs also change. It is hardly surprising to a generation which has seen the rise of the Internet from something almost unknown, to a prominence which makes it a feature of our day-to-day lives. Since the 1980s we have seen the burgeoning of TV channels, satellite and terrestrial, and the development of cheap international phone calls. Regular TV reports from the other side of the world by Satphone are almost as easily achieved as a local call was a quarter of a century ago.

Change is the lifeblood of language, and of local language just as much as of the standard tongue. In the chapters that follow, we shall be charting that change all round the country, from the birth of regional English, over one thousand years ago.

2

ASHINGTON

Previous page: Woodhorn Colliery is on the fringe of Ashington further along the coal seam. This depiction of the colliery was knitted by Mary Preston who has never been out of Ashington. She has knitted many local scenes, brass bands, miners' picnics. The style is very like that of local *proggy* mats which were made from any redundant cloth.

Right: Radically changed, looking fresh as if out of its bath, the pit is more of a social focus, for few men over 50 can find work. The pit is now half museum (employing about 8 people) and half derelict site. You can go into the winding room with its working engines, which turned the evocative huge wheels that dominate the skyline of every pit.

The first thing that strikes you about Ashington is how clean it is. This is a tidy place with green lawns, scrubbed brick sheds like oversized signal boxes and a smart little cafeteria. Only the two wheels of the pithead winding gear, one red, the other black, speak unmistakably of the sweaty labour of hewing coal.

Woodhorn Colliery closed in 1981, and in the twenty years since it has become more a museum than a pit. Three miles up the road at Ellington stands the last working pit in the North-East of England. But here at Ashington there is no lowering slag heap of spoil, no coal dust crunching underfoot, no sooty stains down the brickwork of the winding-shed. As we pass, a man hails us from where he sits, his Labrador panting quietly at his feet, to shout tales of his decades working underground here; of pitmen shorn of limbs in horrific accidents in the levels below; of bodies borne out of the shaft by this same winding-gear; of heads crushed by splintering pit-props. There's a long sob in his voice, his speech thick with the old, so-called 'Pitmatic' accents of Ashington. It is as if he must shout out loud the hard truths so that the memory of the lives lost should not vanish completely under the tended lawns and neatly-aligned cars in the Queen Elizabeth II Country Park.

The changing of Ashington, once Northumberland's biggest complex of shafts and levels, is manifest wherever you turn. Now there are industrial parks and shopping centres. The old *raas* or 'rows' of houses have been spruced up and brightly painted. People here no longer spend their lives cutting coal underground, but are engaged in light surface labour or on the dole – unemployment touches 50% round these parts – so the heart is being knocked out of much of the talk. Or that's the way they tell it. If you look up the old word lists that the *Survey of English Dialects* from Leeds University

produced from the North-East in the 1940s, or even a more recent linguistic census for the University of Newcastle, you will find a vocabulary rich in pit-words such as *keeker, keepy-back, duff, at bank, riding the limmers*, but these are now words which belong to the past and have only occasional echoes in the conversation of the average teenager.

At Ashington High School, 15-year-old Adam Davidson looked blankly at us when confronted with these mysterious terms. They meant absolutely nothing to him. *Duff*, to him is 'faulty' or 'broken', and nothing to do with coal dust, and *at bank* meant somewhere you get money, rather than 'on the surface' (as opposed to underground) which is what every old pitman meant. In fact, *duff* was fine, useless coal-dust that accumulated as larger chunks were hewn out of the face, and because it was useless the word 'duff' itself came to mean 'worthless' and then 'faulty', so Adam was not so far off the mark there as at first appeared – he had simply missed out the linguistic transfer and was not aware of the link.

There is not the faintest echo of recognition, either, when the suggestion that Adam (or his brother Dean) might refer to their friends, their mates as their *marras*. This old and well-rooted Northumbrian word for workmate was, as we saw in the first book of *Routes of English*, alive and well-understood by Adam and Dean's exact contemporaries on the other side of the country, just south of the Solway Firth. In Wigton, the old words – not only *marra* (mate) but *stree* (straw/a fork) – were still around and reasonably commonplace. But here in Ashington, they are ancient history to today's teenagers.

The coal from Ashington helped fuel the Industrial Revolution. These young men from the town, Adam and Dean Davidson and Mark Smith, will have to look more to silicon than carbon for their prosperity.

It's not that Adam, Dean and their friend Mark Smith, to whom we also spoke, don't – or can't – 'talk broad'. In fact, quite the opposite. Adam and Dean are particularly interesting in this way. Dean (the eldest of the Davidson children, who is aiming for a teaching career) talks a form of gently accented Received Pronunciation (standard southern English) while Adam, only two years younger, is completely different. His is a staccato delivery full of angular shards of words, many traditional grammatical features of north-eastern English like *us* for 'me', but with few traces of the old Tyneside or mining words, with the exception of *divvent* for 'don't', and after prompting from Dean, a vague recollection of *dunsh* for 'hit' or 'bash'. This may have been a memory of the cars in Newcastle which were once adorned with local bumper stickers that read '*Divvent dunsh us* ['Don't hit me'] – *we're Geordies!'*

Cracket was another word – reported in a BBC survey just under twenty years ago, to be familiar to everybody in the area – which left Adam, Dean and Mark nonplussed. A *cracket* was a 'stool'. Originally the pitman sat on his *cracket* underground to save his knees and his back as he hewed coal from the seam, and soon the *cracket* became a fixture of every Northumbrian home. Yet it meant nothing to Adam, Dean and Mark.

When Adam lets rip, he is incomprehensible. His language is fast, heavily accented ('rough', says his brother) and full of teenage slang. Some of it is local like *mint* for 'good' ('Not like grows on trees and "plantey" like', says Adam. 'No, it's mint, man!') Other words have a wider distribution: *nesh* for 'bad' and *lush* for 'attractive'. He, like Mark, uses *canny* as a useful positive descriptor. 'That's one of the words I tend to use,' says Mark, 'like "oh, she's dead canny" or "oh, he's a canny good teacher". That's something a lot of people say'.

Manny Shinwell – a radical Labour politician born in London but brought up in Glasgow. First elected as MP in 1931, he subsequently got a seat in Durham in 1935 (Seaham Harbour). As Chairman of the Labour Party from 1942 he wrote the manifesto which gave Labour their greatest general election victory of 1945. As Minister of Fuel and Power in 1946 he nationalised the mines and coal industry. There was no-one more suitable to open the famous Ashington Institute in 1930, The 'Tute' provided sports and recreational facilities to the miners for a penny a week and was a major cultural force in the area.

So what's going on here? In its heyday in the 1930s this was one of Britain's most concentrated mining communities, with 6,000 men underground and many of their wives serving in the canteen or doing other jobs *at bank* (on the surface). The miners breathed coal dust together, ate their *bait* (snack) together, depended on one another for their mutual safety, drank together and wedded one another's daughters and sons. The single occupation provided a framework for work and life and gossip and pain and death. Closely-knit is the cliché used of pit-communities, and it is undeniable that these villages were self- sufficient and self-supporting. The pit was at the centre of the village and life itself was measured by its demands.

'It was a macho life', says Raymond Reed, son of the greatest voice of Northumbrian dialect poetry, the late Fred Reed. 'They needed hard words, their own words to express themselves'. And the vocabulary of the pit – 'Pitmatic', which is far richer than merely a list of specialist implements and techniques, provided that means of expression. Pages and pages long is the list of distinct local words, derived from Scots, or at least having common ancestry with Scots, or from old Anglian roots.

Joan Beal works in the department of English Literature and Language at Newcastle University and has made a special study of the structure and evolution of Tyneside speech and 'Pitmatic'. According to her, it is difficult to define exactly the area in which 'Pitmatic' is spoken, but in broad terms it relates to the speech of the old pit villages of the Ashington area, not far from the North Sea coast, half a dozen miles north-west of the market town of Morpeth and a bare dozen or so north of Newcastle-upon-Tyne, the great urban enclave of 'Geordie' speech.

Perhaps if you went as far south as the Northumberland/North Tyneside border, to places

The town came into being very quickly in the middle of the 19th century and the tied houses of the pitmen were built in row after monotonous row. In a house in a typical *raa* the front doors might face each other across minimal gardens with a narrow public path, all rarely used. You went in by the unlocked back door via the scullery. The toilets were outside with the *cree*, the coal house for the pitmen's free coal concession, which might be traded with non-miners.

like Cramlington and Dudley, where there once were pits which have long since closed, you would find older people who speak quite similarly to the people of Ashington. If you go west as far as Morpeth, you're hitting a big market town with a much more genteel population and they wouldn't speak like that there. So I would say it's in this corner of south Northumberland that was the site of the once great south Northumberland coalfield, that you have this dialect which is locally known as 'Pitmatic', but which is, in fact, simply a better preserved Northumbrian than you would find in the urban Tyneside area.

It is a strange word, 'Pitmatic'. The first time I encountered the term, I almost had to rub my ears. The suffix -matic suggests something more to do with machinery than language, by analogy with 'automatic'. It seems to be a straightforward coinage, which is almost certainly nineteenth-century.

It's a word that sort of makes a dialect of the language of the pit. The other term of course is *yakker* – *pit yakker*. *Yakker*'s obviously from a word meaning to talk, but you will also hear people talk about *yakker* as the kind of language you have here. And of course 'Pitmatic' isn't confined to this area, there's also a 'Durham Pitmatic', which is different.

Mining started in the North-East of England in the eighteenth century and at that time, physical boundaries were a real barrier – the sea, of course, to the east was one, but also hills to the west and north, and the *River Tees* was a cut-off southwards. For the poor Victorian miner, sweating his life out at the dangerous levels of the Northumbrian coalfield, the village with its tight knit community was almost as far as he strayed. As **Joan Beal** went on to say:

The pit village was almost manufactured to create the kind of very tight social networks which tend to preserve traditional ways of speech. In the pit village, the pit *raas* (the

houses built in the rows for the pit workers to live in) meant that you necessarily lived next door to the people you worked with. You had the Miners' Social Club, so you socialised with the people that you worked with. I had a student from Ashington who told me that until she was nine years old she never played with another child who wasn't her cousin. This was because there was this very close-knit network of family and friends, and that tends to reinforce traditional values. Where you have very close-knit networks, you get the traditional norms of language as well as other kinds of activity reinforced. I think the pit village is just that kind of network.

So we find a considerable assortment of pit-terms that together make up 'Pitmatic'. Not all of them are words with independent meanings. The dictionaries and word-lists are filled with strange-looking words *(raas, wark, clivvor)* that are simply the way the list-maker has represented the 'Pitmatic' pronunciation of standard English words (rows, work, clever). But many are individual terms that breathe the life of the pit: *hoggers* (trousers), *keepy-back* (savings), *bobby-ends* (discarded pieces of pit-props), *chummuns* (empty coal-tubs), *keeker* (colliery-overseer), *howk* (pull, dig) *kist* (pit-deputy's chest) and so on.

Both at home and at play, the word-list reflects common preoccupations: *marra* (mate), *hoppins* (fair), *cowp ya creels* (do a somersault), *palatic* (drunk), *shuggyboats* (fairground swingboats), *tab* (cigarette), *play the wag* (play truant), *tappy-lappy* (at top speed), *bait* (snack, packed lunch), *stotty-cake* (flat cake of bread), *kizzen* (overcook), *netty* (earth-closet) etc.

So where did the dialect of this part of the world originate? **Paul Foulkes**, a language researcher at the University of Leeds, who has been making a special study of north-eastern talk, had some interesting comments:

When I was living in Newcastle, I had some Danish friends visit me and the first thing I did was warn them that they might find it difficult to understand the locals but, in fact, they actually found it easier than anywhere else. It's almost as if Geordie and Danish formed a continuum. There is a strong influence from the Norse, certainly on the vocabulary: words like *flit* (to move) come straight from old Norse. And place names have also got a strong influence from Norse.

However **Joan Beal** feels that the Scandinavian connection can be overstated. She says the roots of the local language are much more deeply planted in the Old English tradition (Anglian – a dialect of which was spoken in this area), as opposed, for instance, to Yorkshire dialect where Scandinavian settlements produced a much richer word horde.

You do get some words from Scandinavian. In Woodhorn Colliery museum, for instance, they have a *kist*, which is the sort of desk that the foreman worked at, and that's the Scandinavian form of 'chest'. But I think one of the things that people are very proud of about the vocabulary here is its ancientness, the fact that it goes back to old English times. And so you tend to get preserved in Northumbrian words like *bairn* which are Old English words – they're not Scandinavian – that have died out in other parts of the country.

Bairns for children is, of course, preserved in standard Scots, but is no longer used in English. Similarly the local Northumbrian word *burn* for a stream is Anglian and goes back to the dawn of the English language in this part of the world. According to Joan Beal, evidence of how people actually spoke a thousand years ago in the settlements

Mining terminology

The northern coal mines had many words and expressions peculiar to themselves which were called **pitmatic**.

Colliers were the ships in which coal was transported to London and elsewhere in the UK. The **viewer** was the manager of a colliery and the **deppity** (deputy) was the man in charge of a section of a mine. A **stoneman** built stonepacks to keep the roof of the seam up. A **marra** was a young boy who pushed a tub of coal. Marras usually worked in pairs, one pushing and the other pulling. Those who worked down the pit were called **pitmen, yakkers** or **crankies** or **howkies. Shiftwork** was any work not done at a **piecework** rate.

The **cavil** was the system used to distribute, by lot, the work places in the pit.
The two-foot gauge railway that ran through the miles of tunnels underground was known as the **transit**. The small open wagons were known as **tubs**. Transit workers kept the tubs on the move. A **filler** was part of a team that attacked a 100 yard seam of coal with picks and shovels throwing coals onto a conveyor belt. A **putter** was a young man who worked with a pit pony to supply the fillers with empty tubs. A **drawer** went in after the fillers had taken out the coal and drew out the chocks which sent the roof crashing to the floor. The **cutterman** used a cutting machine to cut a wedge of coal from the bottom half of the seam to enable the fillers to have easier access: a dangerous job that claimed many lives.

Drooned-oot refers to a mine that had been flooded.
Duff was coal dust.
Galloway was a breed of pony often used in mines.
Hoggers were footless stockings worn by pitmen at work, which enabled grit etc to be extracted more easily.
Jowl was to strike a wall in the pit as a signal especially when trapped below to attract rescuers.
Keekerb was an overlooker at a pit whose main job was to examine the coals as they came out of the pit.
Laid-in was a pit that had ceased working because the coal was exhausted.

of Northumberland is scanty. Caedmon's Hymn, written in the eighth century, in the venerable Bede's *History*, is one piece of documentary evidence which reveals the local use of *barn* (modern bairn). By the sixteenth century the same word was detectable in a work written in London called *A dialogue both pleasant and pitiful against the fever pestilence*. Joan Beal says the work portrays an Elizabethan stereotype of the Northumbrian:

...a character called Mendicus, a beggar, who is supposed to be from Northumberland, uses this word *barns*, which probably at that time would have been pronounced bairns – 'me and my bairns' and that picks him out to an Elizabethan London audience as a Northumbrian.

Outside influence has also marked the speech of the area, though this development came a century after the character Mendicus lampooned the local way of talking. Hitherto, the region was seen as fairly isolated, 300 or more miles from London and circumscribed by physical boundaries. The catalyst for change was the Industrial Revolution and the need for coal to fire it. **Dominic Watt**, who works alongside Paul Foulkes at Leeds University, sets the scene:

Newcastle was probably until the seventeenth century a very small and fairly insignificant place, but it became the first coal-mining town in England, perhaps one of the first in the world. It was really when the coal mining started that the need for labour to work in the mines brought people flooding into the area. They came from all over the north of England and also from Scotland, from Ireland, from Wales and even the southern counties of England to work in the mines, and later they would work in other industries, too, like shipbuilding, (a fact the writer Daniel Defoe commented on in his travels around the north of England).

In this isolated and mixed community, where heavy industry occupied and consumed the working and recreational lives of all its inhabitants, there grew up one of the most expressive local languages in the United Kingdom – Geordie, with its local rural variants. One of the features that is testimony to the vigour and richness of this local language is its well developed grammar. As **Joan Beal** said:

Grammar is what really makes a dialect a dialect, rather than simply standard English with a different accent. The fact that you do have grammatical patterns, that are really quite distinct from standard English, in this part of the country, makes it very interesting and sometimes can cause misunderstandings. One of the most intriguing features of the grammar here is what we call the 'double modal' verb.

Modal verbs in English are verbs like 'shall', 'can', 'may' and 'must', and in standard English the rule is that only one can stand within a sentence. So you can say 'I shall come tomorrow' but 'I must shall come tomorrow' is ungrammatical.

In this part of the country, though, you can have two modals in a sentence. Not any old combination – they are restricted. For instance, I met a lady from Stakeford (another little former mining village near Ashington on the road to Morpeth) and I heard her say, 'But you must can do it'. And this made me take a step back.

Now what makes it particularly interesting is that this is the only dialect within England in which you have that combination. You find it in Scotland, and in the Appalachian Mountains in America. So it's only the Scots and the Hillbillies – and the Geordies, or rather the Northumbrians – who use this combination.

Chaucerian English is what Ashington talk most resembles in another of its grammatical features, since the past participle of a range of verbs takes the suffix -en in the past. So it is quite normal to hear *putten* for 'put' ('he 's putten the coal on the fire') and, instead of 'I've got one', 'I've *getten* a one'. Note how this is very like, though not the same as, the American *gotten*. Another grammatical feature that marks out the talk of this corner of England from standard English is the pronominal system. The pronouns of Geordie dialect are both very different from the standard language and at the same time so systematic in their application, that Joan Beal is able to draw up a table of usage.

It appears in many ways to be a simple reversal of the norm: so instead of saying 'give it to us', locals would say 'give it *wuh*', (where wuh is simply a pronunciation of 'we'). And it is much less likely that you'd hear *us* as the subject form, although it does occur ('us'll do that').

That's what we call pronoun transfer and I've seen it alleged that this is something that only happens in the South-West of England because they do it much more in the South-West, with 'him' and 'her' and so on, but it does occur here. And in the North-East, of

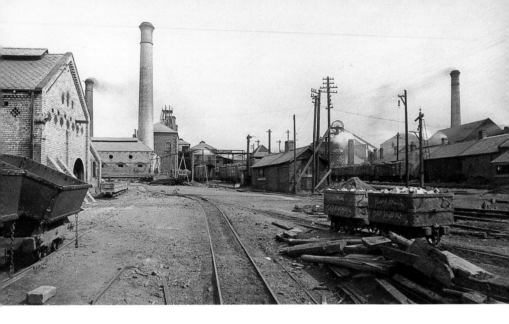

course, 'us', also means 'me'. So 'give it us' means 'give it to me'. And if you were talking about more than one person, you'd say 'give it we'. So you get a sort of transfer of forms that you would normally get in standard English.

With the pronoun 'you', Ashington talk retains an audible difference between singular and plural, nominative and accusative (subject and object) usage which has been completely lost from mainstream English. Joan continued:

What I'm describing here is an innovation – dialect's not static – it's not something that's ancient. I think it is something that needs to be asserted, that dialects are often superior to standard English. So, for example, standard English has lost the ability to distinguish between 'you' meaning 'you' (singular), and 'you' meaning 'more than one' (Tyneside: *yous*). So I've heard my daughter say 'Are yous going out tonight?' meaning are both myself and my husband going out, is she going to have the house to herself. And in the really refined versions you even hear people saying *ye*, to one person when it's the subject, so 'ye can go'. The form *you* is used when it's the object – 'I'll give it you'. *Yees* is the subject or nominative plural form: 'yees can gang', 'you (plural) can go', and *ye* and *yous* for the object – 'I'll give it yous'. So there you have a sort of perfect set of pronouns whereas in standard English you only have 'you'. Now that is actually an innovation, that's something that came in the nineteenth century.

One of the linguistic consequences that we have remarked upon elsewhere in these books is that when a specialist vocabulary draws much of its strength from an evolving tradition, it is vulnerable. In Cumbria, our youngsters debated hotly the currency of *gripe* (three-pronged fork), as the object itself has been superseded. And in

Ashington colliery *c*. 1910. The pits employed 5000 of the town's 25,000 population. It gave them not only wages but houses and coal, and the Miners' Institute – the 'Tute' – which was their pub. Their work and social life had no boundary between them. The closing of the colliery has not brought the demise of the town, many people have stayed and many others have moved in from neighbouring Newcastle. The pit may have killed many miners but its death has not killed the town.

Ashington, what has happened elsewhere as tractor replaced horse, and farming became an industry, has now happened to the coal industry.

It was almost unthinkable. An industry as old as anyone could remember, that underwrote, not just manufacturing in Britain, but the whole Industrial Revolution, has been routed. British coal was what made the workshop of the world work. Coal for steam, coal for blast furnaces, coal for electricity, coal to keep the home fires burning. To study the industrial geography of Britain, even as late as the 1960s, was to define the nation's regions in terms of its coalfields, laid out across the map like patches on the flank of some brindled cow.

So to take out the coal industry was so unthinkable that the signs were not read. Ecological signs, cost signs, geological signs were. Seams became worked out, traditional industries abandoned British coal as a fuel source and 'Pitmatic' was breathing its last. Because the rule is unerring and inevitable: as the craft dies or is replaced, so the craftspeak dies along with it. **Joan Beal** also said:

I think there's a general trend, which we've also observed in Tyneside dialect, for what's called 'levelling'. The very particular dialectal characteristics are smoothed off, so that there's a sort of local standard emerging. Now I think what you will find here is that, because we no longer have the pits, that very close-knit way of life has tended to break down. I think among the older people it is still there because they still have the social clubs, they still have the allotments, they still have their leek clubs and they would probably live the same kind of life. But what do the younger people do? Where do they go for their entertainment? Do they go into Newcastle?

The question itself points to a swiftly changing culture. To reflect and describe this changing world, new local usages are forging their way on to the linguistic map. *Lush* and *nesh* may have a geographical currency which goes further than the North-East, yet how familiar are these terms beyond a certain age-group? Maybe Adam Davidson's *mint* for 'good' is not only a young-person's term, but local too. Not every London teenager would recognise it.

There seem to be new ways of defining local talk, though strong local pronunciation and some regional words still play their part. **Dr Clive Upton**, of Leeds University, runs the *Survey of English Dialects*, the sixty-year old study of the way local English is evolving. He talked about dialect in England today:

If you think of dialects as being minute differences village-by-village, then certainly they are 'dying out', because to an extent you've got regional standards developing over quite large areas. But as long as you accept that definition of a dialect as being a form of speech that's set off from another form of speech by a complex of grammar, pronunciation, and lexis, they are alive and well. And given the fact that we have a much greater social mix than we ever did hitherto and that people are much more mobile in many ways too, a lot of new elements are coming in to speech which we need to take account of which didn't exist before.

Raymond Reed is quite elderly now. He writes poetry and, like his father, speaks broad Pitmatic. As is quite normal at the start of the twenty-first century, he has a number of different degrees or levels of broadness which he can draw upon, ranging from accented standard English through to a full and extreme form of local talk, peppered with old pit-terms. This ability to select an appropriate register – linguists call it 'code-switching' – is a sink-or-swim solution for those who speak broad naturally, but today must be able to converse with a wider world.

My dialect is bi-lingual. I can *taak* or I can 'talk', depending on the person to whom I'm talking. Talking now, I'm answering a question which was asked in standard English, and I wouldn't talk the broad version of Pitmatic because I only use it when I'm talking to me friends, the people I was brought up with, the people I played football with, cycled with, the people I still talk to now, pass the time of day, have a crack. Being bi-lingual in the dialect I think is the most important aspect, because communication is all that matters, and if you speak you must be understood. So this is the best I speak, even though you can tell by me vowel sounds and the inflection in me voice that I'm from round here.

Yet when he is talking to old friends, Raymond becomes very broad and speaks pure Pitmatic:

It was used by men who did a very heavy, macho job. The whole way of life was very masculine. They had a filthy, dirty job, they wore filthy dirty clothes after the first five minutes of the shift, and when I was young there were no pit baths, the men had to just bath in a tin bath, often in front of the fire or in the back end, and it was very difficult to get themselves perfectly clean. And I think the Pitmatic dialect related to this machoism, a sort of an uninhibited machoism. And many of dialect words and expressions in Pitmatic came direct from the pit – for instance the footballer Jackie Milburn never 'scored a hat trick', he 'scored three goals off the belt end'. And the bloke who lived at the end of the street who 'wasn't all there', he 'wasn't a full tub'. And ye never used to say to anybody 'take five' or 'have a rest', you'd say 'tek your pipe till the reek runs oot' – that was the powder reek (smell) down the pit, after it had been used to fire the coal, to stop it.

If a miner was talking to somebody close to him, he might say *warkin* (walking) – 'I'm going warkin'. But if he was talking to one of his *marras* (mates) from the pit he'd probably say 'I'm gan waakin', *waakin* – it was more distinctive, it was stronger. And I got

the impression when I was young that this very very strong version of the dialect was used because it was masculine and powerful. I think this type of modest machoism was very important to them, where they weren't seen to show weakness at all.

Raymond Reed has watched as pits like Woodhorn have closed and with his acute ear for the local talk all around him, he has monitored the levelling that linguists Joan Beal and Clive Upton have picked up in their academic investigations. According to Raymond, television, pop culture and drug culture are modifying the vocabulary of the young – 'crack' is more likely to mean 'cocaine' to a youngster, even in Ashington, he says, than what he knew it as, a talk with friends.

And because a lot more young people don't bother going to school – I hear them when I'm sitting talking to me friends – their command of English is so bad that their vocabulary seems to consist of about twenty-five or thirty words. And you very rarely hear them speak in normal phrases, or sentences: they're speaking in a staccato, machine gun-type voice. Unfortunately a lot of people associate this with the dialect, but it isn't part of the dialect as I know it. The normal Pitmatic is very vibrant, strong, onomatopoeic and expressive, whereas to hear a lot of people speak, especially the younger ones, they'll just grunt and they seem to have their own type of speak.

To listen to **Adam** and **Dean Davidson**, Raymond's comments seem to have some truth. Dean criticises his brother for 'talking rough', and Adam admits that his mother tries to correct the way he speaks. His speech is heavily accented, very rapid, with many elisions and glottal stops that make it hard for the untrained ear to understand readily. It is hard too – as with much dialect, essentially a spoken language form – to render

Miners at North Walbottle Colliery, Newcastle. You can take the miners out of the pits but you cannot take the pit out of the miners. The language of their trade remained in their speech, both in coined words and ordinary words given special meanings. *He wasn't a full tub* meant 'he was a bit thick.' Down the pit a *chummun* was an empty tub, but outside *standing chum* meant your beer glass was empty. *Keep yer poowder dry* referred to miners taking their explosives down the pit and wet powder was no good to them. It is used now to say 'cheerio'.

But much of the language will die with this generation, as there will be no need to refer to objects and actions no longer part of their lives. Though ghosts will remain in common speech for future etymologists to tease out their derivation.

well on the page. To get a better idea of just how dense Adam's way of talking can be, sample the extract from his interview on the accompanying CD. But this short extract, in which Adam describes how he gets told off for the way he speaks, gives an idea of the 'staccato, machine-gun' delivery that Raymond Reed referred to. We have left unedited his false-starts and hesitations which add to the broken quality and its distance from standard English:

Well I get, I get bitten at every time I say something like summat ... like five different, you know if it's not like to their liking or like if I'm not at their standard of speaking I get ... for it or something. But, like if I'm if I'm oot with my friends and naebody tells you that, do they? Like ... you know ... your friends aren't going to say 'Oh stop, you don't speak like that'. And I'm like, we just ... like ... speak the way we want to. We're friends, and if wor parents are there, like the parents might say something, but we'll just come back and speak their ... basically we take no notice of them.

This is not levelling in any way that I can recognise. Adam's is a very strong local accent, liberally peppered with words that are distinctly Geordie at least. He uses *divvent* and *divna* for 'don't' and *wor* for 'our' and other words which are certainly limited in their distribution (like *lush, canny, mint, chava, belter* and the ritual, apparently meaningless, addition of the word 'how' at the end of a phrase). If he is unaware of the pit terms that are at the heart of traditional Pitmatic, that is simply because he no longer has any connection with the 'macho' working life of miners that Raymond Reed recalls.

Local talk

Foreigners – that is, people from places like Sunderland, Yorkshire or even London, **can** make themselves understood in a basic fashion or, with even greater difficulty, understand native Ashingtonians. However, you will ease your stay in the area by learning a few local words and phrases.

Divvent, sorry, don't, assume Ashingtonian is English pronounced differently. Many of the words are completely different and students of Chaucer or Old English will be at a distinct advantage as will Scandinavians.

The Geordie diphthong is not minuscule swimming attire, rather it is a moment of indecision when you can't decide which of two vowels to pronounce so you sound both. For example, *The beyor at hyem is not byad* – The beer at home isn't bad.

Your voice should rise at the end of each sentence, but no more than an octave.
Each 'R' should b pronounced as if there were 10 there or as if you are going to clear your throat (originally of coal dust) If you wish to really amuse the inhabitants pronounce 'bath' as if there was a R in it.

His brother **Dean**, two years older and not far off RP, does not like the way Adam and others like him from Ashington talk:

I think it does sound very rough to me; it does sound really rough. And it doesn't sound very, very attractive how people speak in Ashington, to other people watching them on TV.

However, **Adam** is fiercely proud of his own area and wears his talk like a badge of honour that represents Ashington:

I'm an Asher he says, Stakeford is just a mile doon the road, and we call 'em Stakies and they call us Ashers. Like, if there's one Asher and a load of Stakies, you know you want to get runnin', because basically we divvent like each other. We're different like.

So what are we to conclude about the state of health of the local talk around Ashington at the start of the new century? Certainly change is afoot. Yet there is not a corner of the English language where development is not taking place. Maybe that change is happening at a faster rate, propelled in this community by the wholesale closure of pits like Woodhorn over the past twenty years or so, which has excised a whole swath of localised and specific pit-talk from routine use. But as we discover all along the very local routes of English that we are tracing in this book, much of the evidence is contradictory. And for every tale of levelling out of local linguistic particularities towards more of a regional standard, you can find another of fierce local pride in the distinctive talk of a specific community, as expressed so forcefully by the youngster Adam with his sticking-up for his fellow *Ashers*. As Leeds University researcher **Paul Foulkes**

These are some of the phrases you may hear:

Yous aa'd better gan canny – You (plural) had better take care walking here.

Wor lass, giz a piece a cyek in me bait? – Darling, may I have a piece of cake in my packed lunch?

If ye slip in the clarts ye could well cowp yor creels – Should you slip on the mud you may go head over heels.

Wor da will taak yer bairns te the footy – My Dad will take your children to the football match.

Yous is getten ne stotty cyek fer yer suppa – You will not be having any stotty-cake (local bread) for your dinner.

Gizza bottle o' broon, geordie – May I have a brown ale please, sir.

Divvent hoy yer dottle inna netty – Do not dispose of the remains of your cigarette in the public convenience.

observes, evidence of change always needs to be handled with care:

Varieties are not fixed entities. All speakers of all languages have a natural repertoire of different styles, different pronunciation forms, different vocabulary forms, different syntactic forms, which they can use for particular purposes. And those include different styles for talking to other locals, different styles for talking to people who are clearly not local, different styles for talking to people who are not even native speakers.

Dialect experts like **Clive Upton** and Stanley Ellis, whose whole working lives have been spent charting the ups and downs of the dialect map of the United Kingdom also urge caution:

No language – dialect, standard English or whatever – is static, and dialect is moving on, it's dropping words. Certainly the vocabulary's going, not just because of influence of the cities but largely because the items themselves are going. But that doesn't stop you identifying almost instantly the pronunciation of a man who's lived in a district all his life and as soon as he opens his mouth you're pretty sure that he comes from that place just over the hill, or far in another country.

3

DERRY

There are few places in Britain whose name alone can inspire hatred and division, or where the way you describe your home town can be seen as a political and historical statement. That is the case with the second city of Northern Ireland – Londonderry to one section of its inhabitants, Derry to another.

It is true that divided communities or allegiances are also to be found elsewhere in the United Kingdom. There are, for instance, the rival football teams supported by one or another community within the same city – Liverpool and Everton, Celtic and Rangers. Yet to make a politico-linguistic statement by the way you refer to a place is something else again.

That becomes a big problem when broadcasting impartiality comes into the picture. It obliged the staff of the little BBC local radio station of Foyle (named after the river that flows through the city and thus in name resolutely non- sectarian) to think very carefully about how they referred to their city on air. A policy was required. So today the rule is that the first reference in any broadcast is to Londonderry and thereafter to Derry. But live broadcasters can be quixotic souls and so the idiosyncratic morning radio host on Foyle, Gerry Anderson, decided to come up with his own brand of evenhandedness whereby he regularly referred to the city as 'Derry/Londonderry' – or, in spoken form 'Derry-stroke-Londonderry'.

Perhaps inevitably, through endless repetition 'Derry-stroke-Londonderry' came to sit uncomfortably on the lips of the disc-jockey. So Gerry just took an axe to it, creating the celebrated 'Stroke City'. In so naming the town he simultaneously created a wry joke about the place. Because Derry is a very particular place, and **Gerry Anderson** – a Derry man born and bred – should know:

Ireland in the Seventeenth Century

During the seventeenth century the Catholics in Ireland rebelled strongly against the English Protestant rule which was being imposed on them. When he ascended the throne, King James I realised that he had to do something to suppress this rebellion and he set about the 'plantation' of Ulster, which meant that he selected suitable areas of land, drove the native Irish people away from it and 'planted' English Protestant settlers in their place. This was done in different stages and appeared at the time to be an effective solution but it created lasting problems for both Protestants and Catholics, which even now remain unsolved. These are some of the important dates in the struggle between Catholics and Protestants:

1607 James I starts the 'plantations' of English families on Irish land.

1618 The plantation of Derry – a major project organised by the London livery companies

1641 Irish Catholics took advantage of Charles I's problems in England and raised an armed rebellion in Ulster

1641 Cromwell decided to put down rebellion in Ireland. He landed in Dublin and launched an attack on Drogheda where he is said to have caused the death of 2,000 citizens.

1688 James II, who was a Catholic, was deposed from the English throne and the Protestant William of Orange became King. James fled to Ireland and raised an army to fight William's forces and win back the crown.

1689 James II and his army besieged the city of Derry for 105 days. Twenty thousand Protestants were within the city of whom about 7,000 died of disease or starvation before relief came from England.

1690 William of Orange finally defeated James II at the Battle of the Boyne. This victory led to the suppression of Irish Catholicism for 300 years and is still celebrated every year by the Orangemen of Northern Ireland.

This is a very feisty kind of a town – the people are very feisty because everything seems to begin and end here. Troubles begin here before they begin anywhere else and they end here before they end anywhere else. Everything seems to happen here. I don't know why. It's the people; the people have been described as, well, nasty; they've also been described as cantankerous; they've been described as very tight communities; they've been described as generous; they've been described as musical; in fact they've been described as everything...

The city was originally just called 'Derry', or more accurately *Doire* in the Irish language, meaning 'oak grove'. The oak trees that gave their name to the city grew on an island in the *River Foyle*, whose marshy shallows, the Bogside, became famous as the site of some of the most violent sectarian struggles of the twentieth century. *Doire* acquired the blessing of the great sixth-century Irish saint, St Columba (*Colmcille* in

Left: Sir Cahir O'Doherty's sword. O'Doherty was a Gaelic Chieftain who led an unsuccessful uprising against the English Protestants in 1608 in which Derry was burnt. This gave the Protestants an opportunity to build a fortified walled area in Derry and further extended English social and economic influence.

Right: The Seige of 1689. Since the accession of James II, there had been a consistent policy of replacing Protestants with Catholics in leading positions in the administration and army in Ireland.The arrival of a new garrison at Derry and rumours of a planned massacre of the Protestant population threw the city into panic. The young apprentice boys of the city closed the city's gates.

Derry's very small and in a sense everybody lives cheek-by-jowl here, no matter what kind of background you come from. And I suppose the walled city is the City of Londonderry – the English colonial city of Londonderry – which was 'planted' here (the word actually used was 'planted') in the seventeenth century on top of, if you like, the Gaelic and the medieval. And so the English or the Protestants – the colonists – were *within* the walls and the natives, the Catholics, the Irish were outside the walls. And that juxtaposition is still there right to this very day.

It came dramatically into play in 1969 with the Apprentice Boys – one of the Orange or 'Loyal' Protestant institutions that annually marched around the walls. In that year, as the political tensions were rising, this is where the Protestant marchers and the Catholic young people came into conflict once and for all. And that was in effect the beginning of the Troubles.

Londonderry as a name defies all the normal principles and practice of linguistic development. Words tend to get abbreviated, not lengthened. But then this is Ireland and Ireland is a special case – always.

Although Derry is a neater and, as we have seen, a more historically accurate way to name the city, that does not cut any ice with those who consciously reject nationalist Ireland and who stress every connection with the colonising power, England. Loyalists – for whom the monumental city wall, complete and unbroken, is the physical symbol of historic English power – systematically reject the naked Derry. For them to say Londonderry is not a polysyllabic inconvenience, but a useful shorthand. In one word it defines not only the city but the speaker's place in it.

In the long run, and while real peace seems still a long way off, **Gerry Anderson**'s 'Stroke City' seems a pretty good bet. As he says:

You've got two completely different sets of people, with completely different backgrounds, completely different cultures, completely different languages who actually should've integrated with each other four hundred years ago and that just didn't happen. It's as if the seventeenth century meets the twenty-first with a bang.

But beyond the mere matter of what the city is called, the linguistic geology of Derry is a complex system of layers and beds, overlaid and contorted by waves of settlement and political allegiance. In the first series of *The Routes of English* we met **Dr Loreto Todd** – an Ulsterwoman from County Tyrone – at the Pierhead in Liverpool, where she showed us how Irish speech had helped define the shape of modern Scouse. When we encountered her for a second time, she was at home in her office at the University of Leeds where she is Honorary Reader in International English at the department of English Language. We asked her to do a bit of excavation of the linguistic strata of Northern Ireland:

In a way Northern Ireland is unique. You have a mixture of English varieties that are found no place else in exactly that quantity. I think it was the Northern Ireland poet Tom Paulin who said that when you look at a language you can see all sorts of layers, and interactions and so on. If you think in terms of Northern Ireland and just go back a thousand years, you've got the Irish Gaelic speakers from Northern Ireland interacting with the Gaelic speakers from Scotland, interacting with the Viking settlers who came, interacting with the Lowland Scots who came, interacting with the English who came, and with the Welsh and producing that type of composite. Similar composites exist in other parts of the world but not quite that particular mixture. That's not to say that you get homogeneity throughout the six counties of Northern Ireland – you certainly do not. Each area is either subtly or sharply differentiated from each other. But you certainly can say that, even in an island like Ireland, there are differences between the north and the south.

For **Sam Burnside**, who works in Derry with the Verbal Arts Centre, the speech of the city has a wealth of linguistic colours that derive not only from its ancestral and colonial history but also from its geographical situation and industrial heritage. English, Irish and Ulster Scots – the three linguistic traditions that run through the language of the city – are, as he points out, so intertwined as to be virtually impossible for the layman to untangle.

But I think the accumulation of riches that flow from those three in our culture is the love for language and a sense of the music of language. And I think that's still with us.

Although the northern part of Ireland is small, there are quite distinct differences from place to place. Even a few miles outside Derry you find pockets of communities where there are very Scots intonations and others where there would be very strong English intonations, because the city of Derry had been Irish-speaking initially, then the Plantation came along in the 17th century. That brought English and Scottish into this area. Then, because the city of Derry was also a port with people going out and people coming in constantly, there was a great kaleidoscope of words, of languages and so on. But then layered on top of that was the fact that the city was also a dock – the docks were here. There was an industrialised city in terms of shirt-making – the shirt industry – and those kind of working conditions develop and stimulate a type of language that is very abrupt, with very short sentences.

For example, if you met a Derry person on the street you might say 'Hello', and he or she would say *'Bout you*! which means 'About you!' …which means 'How about you?' or 'How are you today?' It's a speech pattern that has to take account of working conditions, where people are rushed, there's lots of noise and so on. All these influences have produced a speech pattern in Derry that's quite distinct from little villages five or ten miles away

The language of Ireland has been powerfully shaped by the ebb and flow of the island's turbulent history, the geographical origins of the population marking the speech of their descendants for generations. To see how this evolved, let us turn the clock back a thousand years to the traditional starting-point for our journeys along *The Routes of English*. In England at that time (as we saw in Book 1) there were four main dialects of Old English quartering up the kingdom, of which the dominant one, spoken in the then capital, Winchester, was West Saxon. Celtic Wales and Cornwall would have been largely peopled by non-English speakers, and likewise, across the water to the west, Ireland was entirely Irish Gaelic speaking. But, says **Dr Loreto Todd**, there were always regional variations:

Even in those days, Northern Ireland Irish was different from south of Ireland Irish – south of Ireland Gaelic – and very similar to the Gaelic that was spoken in the Western Isles and the Scottish Highlands. The link between Northern Ireland and Scotland has existed certainly for 1500 years, and was quite strong even a thousand years ago. So the people in Northern Ireland, in Derry for example, would, if they had been contacted by Highlanders or islanders, have been able to understand them. There were differences of course, but it was a bit like people in the north of England understanding each other a little bit better than they would have understood people from a hundred or two hundred miles away. So there would have been inter-intelligibility between the two. So the link with Scotland has always been very strong.

And Ireland would have no doubt remained Irish-speaking had it not been for the conquering English, who not only colonised the island but brought their powerful language with it. The result was the development in the south of Ireland of Hiberno-English, a specific dialect which owes many of its distinctive flavours and grammatical

Boy and girl at Cahera. The
Irish Famine as depicted in
the *Illustrated London News.*

structures to the underlying bedrock of Irish and which constitutes the heart of today's
Irish variety of English. In the north, the plantation policy of the sixteenth and
seventeenth centuries that underpinned the British hold on Derry, firmly planted the
English language too. As **Dr Loreto Todd** points out, however, there is evidence that the
language already had some currency in the area during the 1400s.

**There was definitely some English in Northern Ireland because one of the O'Neills in the
fifteenth century forbade its use in parts of Tyrone. Now you don't have to forbid the use
of something if it's not there, so undoubtedly there was some English there already. But
certainly from the seventeenth century, there's been a lot of English in the area. And
Derry, as a port and as a city, lost its Irish earlier than the surrounding rural areas, since
country people tend to be infinitely more conservative than town dwellers. In town, it was
more expedient for people to speak English.**

However, despite the fact that the Irish could for centuries put up 'English spoken'
notices in shops in Derry, the English language did not prevail for many years. Until the
middle of the nineteenth century, the mother tongue of the majority of the population
was still Irish Gaelic. One of the factors causing upheaval to the language, as to all
aspects of life in Ireland, was the Great Potato Famine of the 1840s, which caused
desperate hardship, social breakdown and waves of emigration. Survival, for many
people, meant emigration to Britain or North America and that meant adopting English.
Yet the turbulent times did not drive out Gaelic. Just how widely English was spoken
and how deeply entrenched Irish remained is often deliberately misrepresented within
British census returns of Ireland. That makes it difficult to get a clear picture. As

Up the Town On Me Own

It was a wil' col' day
and I asked me friends
to go up to the town,
they told me to catch meself on,
so I dandered on down.
There was nothing to do and nothing to see,
so I went to the toilet to do a pee,
I was so wrecked 'cause I'd done a fart,
I was broke to the bone
and I ran home
and that's the last time
I'll go up the town on me own.

Dr. Loreto Todd said:

Languages often die more slowly than they're thought to die. And though the Great Famine of the 1840s certainly had a catastrophic effect on the language, there would have been a lot of Gaelic spoken, say, in the mid-nineteenth century. And you still find pockets of Gaelic speakers in Northern Ireland even as recently as the 1960s.

Today however, it is not Gaelic that you hear shouted out in greetings across the streets of Derry, nor is it Gaelic that the girls of Catholic Thornhill School in the city naturally speak to one another, but a lively and distinctively flavoured variety of English. Above is a poem written and spoken by 13-year-old **Cathy McDermott**.

Dandered, catch meself on, broke to the bone – vivid phrases that bring this poem to life – give it its sharp youthful city bite. This is a powerful and expressive dialect of English. We asked Cathy for a translation:

They told me to 'catch meself on' means just 'do wise up! I'm not going down the town on that sort of a day' like.

'I dandered on down' is like 'I doddled', just sort of 'waddled' – say you're out in the street with your friends, you would say 'do you want to dander – have a wee dander in the shop?'

'I was so wrecked' means that you're really, really embarrassed.

'I was broke to the bone' means 'I couldn't face anybody', 'I couldn't look at anybody', I just had my head down the whole way home, I just couldn't look at anybody and I was afraid to go up the town again because I've done my fart and all.

The traditional wisdom about language in Northern Ireland, where so many characteristics are attributed to one side or the other of the sectarian divide, is that language is neutral. There are no differences of vocabulary, say the experts, no shading of accents between Protestants and Catholics worth mentioning. Some linguists maintain that the pronunciation 'haitch' of the letter 'aitch' is more common amongst the Nationalist community, yet the evidence is slim. New studies, however, are beginning to suggest that the differences are more marked than was at once thought. But if the way you think and vote still only marginally affects the way you speak in Derry, what is the underlying bedrock that has shaped the sound of English in the city? **Dr Loreto Todd**:

You could probably say that there are three fairly marked types of English in Northern Ireland – they overlap and intermingle, of course. The first type is the English of people whose ancestors spoke Irish Gaelic, and that is sometimes referred to as Hiberno-English. The people who spoke Gaelic carried over into the English which they had to learn, their sound patterns, their idioms, their rhythms, their pronunciations – that type of thing. Then you've got Ulster Scots – Scottish people settled in the North of Ireland in huge numbers from the sixteenth, seventeenth centuries on – who brought with them their Lowland Scots, which is still a feature of quite a number of areas in Northern Ireland. And the third type would be the English of people who had come from England in the sixteenth and seventeenth centuries. You can illustrate all of these three separately, but the three communities have lived together for three hundred plus years – even if not always in harmony – and so they have rubbed off on each other.

Dr Kevin McCafferty has made a detailed study of Derry dialect with particular reference to sectarian differences and language.

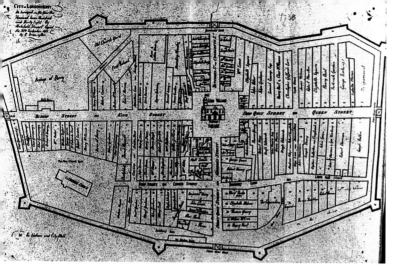

In the Derry area the 'planters' were mainly Scottish. In the seventeenth century Scots outnumbered English settlers there by about twenty to one. So that you would expect some kind of Scottish influence in this area. But that's been modified by contact with other English speakers from other parts of the British Isles, mainly from southern and eastern England, from Cornwall, Devon and London, of course, because Derry was planted from London and the Home Counties by the Guilds of the City of London. And then later on as the Irish population started shifting away from Irish Gaelic towards English you get greater Irish influence, both in the grammar and also in pronunciation.

Just as in Cornwall, you can track the progress of the relations between the indigenous Cornish and the English incomers by looking at the distribution of place names on the map, so, in Northern Ireland, it is the names that uncover your roots.

Often they're hidden, and this is where the idea of having to excavate a language is rather interesting. As you start excavating and taking away the layers, you begin to see that each of these communities has added to what I would regard as a unique amalgam. So you can tell the aboriginal Irish in names like *O'Neill, O'Connell, O'Donnell, McGhie, McGuire*, you can tell the Highlanders in names like *Macdonald, Macdougall, Macduff*. The Lowland Scots in the Paisleys, or the Stuarts, and there are hundreds of these Lowland Scottish families around. English settlers you can spot in names like *Church*, or *Dudley*, or *Ellis*, or *Upton*, or the many names like that.

And you can get little Viking remnants – a name like *McKettrick*, which sounds so Irish and is actually *Mac Hetric – Citric*, 'son of Citric'. Or you get something like *McAuliffe*, which is *Mac Olaf*, 'son of Olaf', or *McLaughlin*, 'son of the settler from the Lakes'.

With a history in Derry of deeply divided traditions – with setbacks for the English colonists followed by settlement designed to subjugate the indigenous people – and religious disagreement, it is little surprise that Derry's social divisions were already clearly mapped long before the start of the most recent unrest or Troubles in 1969. As **Dr Kevin McCafferty** said:

It was one of the most segregated urban areas in the north of Ireland. And that segregation has increased throughout the Troubles. Before 1969, you had quite a lot of Protestants living on the west side of the *River Foyle*; since then about two-thirds of those Protestants have moved across the river into the east bank area known as the Waterside. So that's one reason why you would expect to find linguistic differences of this kind between two communities in a place like this. An already firm division has become even firmer in the last twenty-five years. So you might expect those speech differences to be even more marked amongst the younger generation.

Back at Catholic Thornhill School, the girls are playing it by the book. There is no difference of vocabulary or grammar detectable between Catholics and Protestants, but they can perceive a quality of speaking that is not the same. As one **Thornhill schoolgirl** said:

It's not that you can tell from their accent, but you see over in the Waterside we know that they're Protestants, and the Waterside people don't have such a broad accent as us. They would say their words more properly, if you know what I mean.

Kevin McCafferty's fieldwork in Derry has detected what he considers to be a definite development in the way certain vowels are pronounced, where the local pronunciation of 'border' and 'skirt', for example are – in the Protestant community – shifting away from the traditional Derry pronunciation towards the accent of Belfast.

The young Protestants that I was speaking to might, in terms of identity, be more willing to identify with speakers from Belfast and the east of Northern Ireland as some way of

projecting a Northern Ireland identity, an Ulster identity. Whereas, perhaps, the younger Catholics are more willing to keep their distance from that kind of identity, are not so willing to identify with broadcasters and other figures or authority.

On the other hand, he says, it might just as well be the result of where the young people prefer to hang out and seek entertainment.

There's been a tradition for the last twenty-five or thirty years in Derry for people to go out of the town for entertainment – discos and cinemas – maybe up to forty, fifty miles. Catholics go across the border into Donegal in the Republic of Ireland because the city is right on the border, whereas Protestants are more likely to travel eastwards into the rest of Northern Ireland, so that they might be coming into face to face contact with other people from Belfast, Coleraine, County Antrim, County Down. That's to say from areas where those pronunciations are more widespread than they are in Derry.

Gerry Anderson has a broadcaster's acute ear for subtle differences in pronunciation and vocabulary, and from his radio studio at BBC Foyle is uniquely well placed to monitor them amongst his invisible phone-in callers. He agrees with Kevin McCafferty's findings that amongst the working class, accent differences between Catholic and Protestant are slight, mainly restricted to vowel sounds.

I can't identify where someone lives, by the sound of their voice alone as being from either the west bank of the *Foyle* or the east bank. But once you get into the middle class

Portrait of Bernadette Devlin McAliskey. Another of the Derry Wall murals chronicling major events in the last 30 years in Derry. Bernadette Devlin came to prominence in late 1960s as spokesperson for Catholic rights in Nothern Ireland. The mural shows Bernadette addressing the crowds on the streets of the Bogside. She later received a prison sentence for taking part in and inciting a riot. The bin lids in foreground were used by women and children in the Catholic areas throughout Northern Ireland to alert people of an impending raid by the British Army. The mural is a tribute to the role of women in the civil rights campaign.

it's easier, because middle class Protestants tend to use words that middle class Catholics don't use. Middle class Catholics tend to use a similar vocabulary to working class Catholics. But middle class Protestants tend to use words like 'colleague' and they describe something as being 'fun' and say words like 'tummy' – words you wouldn't hear middle class Catholics use. It's very odd; it's as if middle class Protestants are looking towards England for their reference points, whereas middle class Catholics don't tend to do that.

Gerry Anderson's well-attuned ear and Kevin McCafferty's research work have put some much needed detail into the long-held view that language was one of the few factors that unified the two communities in Northern Ireland. What they have detected is language that is actively and audibly on the move, which is one of the most fascinating aspects of linguistic change. The Great Vowel Shift of the late middle ages may have been hugely radical and altered the audible basic building blocks of how English sounds, but it happened over many years. The sort of evolution that Dr McCafferty is picking up has occured over a period of, at most, thirty years, driven on by political and social allegiances and the desire or the need people have to associate themselves with one or other tradition.

The pronunciation of the phoneme 'th', especially when it occurs in the middle of words, makes **Dr McCafferty's** point very clearly. Take words such as mother, father, brother:

You have quite a widespread feature in Northern Ireland which is to drop the 'th' altogether, and say *moer, fa'er, bro'er*, and *an'or*, instead of 'mother', 'father', brother, 'another' etc. That appears to occur pretty equally across all groups of society. But in Derry you have a second innovation which seems to be a local one, which replaces the 'th'

sound with an 'l' sound. So that you get *moler*, *broler*, *faler*, and *anoler*, and *tegeler* for 'together' and so on. This new pronunciation pattern is much more strongly audible in the Catholic community.

Protestants do not hear it used because they prefer not to go to the places where the people who do use it go. Furthermore, if they are aware of it, they are unlikely to adopt it because of its Catholic associations. Thus Protestants will steer clear of it:

They sort of keep their distance from it and tend not to use it, maybe even regard it as something foreign to them or something wrong. Possibly not consciously – I don't think they would do it consciously.

One of the classic features of southern Irish speech is the expression 'I was *after* doing something' meaning 'I have just done something'. This reputedly is a characteristic that echoes a construction in Gaelic and is often quoted as evidence of the continuing influence of the indigenous Irish language on contemporary English. In Northern Ireland it is another sectarian marker, says **Kevin McCafferty**.

It's often known as the 'hot-news perfect', because it's used to talk about something that has recently happened, or immediately happened before the point of speaking, as in the phrase 'I'm after having a cup of coffee', which is equivalent to standard English 'I have just had a cup of coffee' and it's one of the features that is said to come from Irish Gaelic. There has been one small study from the 1970s that argues that the idiom is a more Western and Catholic feature in Northern Ireland – that's to say, it's much more common in the west of the province than in the east. And it's much more common among Catholics than it is among Protestants.

Also probably originating in Irish Gaelic is the differentiation that can be made by Derry dwellers between habitual actions and the simple present using the form '*I be*'. This, it should be noted, has nothing semantically to do with the west of England form that replaces '*I am*'.

It's the difference that's made in Derry English as in a lot of other types of Irish English between '*I be on the bus*' and '*I'm on the bus*', where '*I be on the bus*' is not the same as '*I am on the bus*'. So that '*I am on the bus*' means '*I'm there now, at this moment*', while '*I be on the bus*' has the force of saying that '*I'm usually on the bus*' or '*I'm often on the bus*' or '*I'm frequently on the bus*'. It's another grammatical feature of Irish English – a habitual tense which might also be carried over from Irish Gaelic.

But if there are a few sectarian features to be picked out of the background blur of the dense passing traffic of Derry language, what strike the incomer are the brilliant colours of the metaphors. It is a quality that unites the language of Derry with the south of Ireland. Gerry Anderson remarks upon it from his standpoint as a sort of traffic cop standing in the middle of the Derry linguistic crossroads. And **Mary Murphy** who came to teach in the city from County Galway, south of the border, was immediately struck by it – it felt like home.

I would imagine that the influence was mainly from the Irish because a lot of the metaphors that were used were the same kind of agricultural metaphors that I would have heard in Galway. Many are taken from the weather and in Derry a lot of the language too was based around, especially, rain. I remember once hearing someone describe a man and she said he had 'enough creases in his face to hold a day's rain'. And everyone here knows exactly what it means, because we've all experienced one whole month of rain.

Dr Loreto Todd agrees that this figurative quality to Derry speech is most likely to originate in Irish-speaking areas:

You'll get it in the use of idioms, for example, that are direct translations – '*as often as fingers and toes*', meaning about twenty times – or similes like '*as light on her foot as a cat at milkin*' – that sort of thing can sound very poetic simply because it's not well known in the general language.

Soon after she moved to Derry back in the early days of the Troubles, **Mary Murphy** was particularly struck by the way one person she knew spoke.

I had a neighbour and she had a wonderful use of language. She said to me one day, 'Mary,' she said, 'did you hear that bomb last night?' And I said 'no I didn't'. And she says 'dear,' she said, 'my husband,' and she always called him by his full name, Paddy Docherty (that wasn't his real name) – 'Paddy Docherty had to be walking with me all night, I was lying like a bleached *corp* in the bed'. What an expression 'a bleached *corp*'! And it was *corp* not 'corpse'. If a word ends in 's' then it's automatically considered to be the plural. So it was a *corp*.

This neighbour was a constant source of entertaining, if occasionally misleading, expressions:

I was constantly in awe of this torrent of language that would come out of Kathleen my friend. Another time she would say 'my husband is very good to me, he *lifts* me and *lays* me.' Now I thought she meant the American meaning of the word 'lay' and I didn't realise that the expression meant giving her a lift in the car – and then *laying* – bringing her back home: *lifting* and *laying*.

She said of a newly married neighbour:

As she rushed through the garden gate to greet her husband when he came home in the evening, she said *'she'd be wrapped around him like a wet flag to a pole'*. And I don't think you can get any closer than that, you know. It's just these amazing graphic descriptions. Everything was figurative and there was a little anecdote embedded in every description. For instance if she wanted to tell me that her brother didn't like fish, where I would maybe say *'my brother doesn't like fish'*, she would say *'see me, see my brother Fred, see fish, he hates it'*. And suddenly it turned into a little story. So I am very aware of the richness of the language here and the dry ironic wit embedded in it and it's totally unselfconscious.

As unselfconscious perhaps as the Derry restaurant which Gerry Anderson spotted advertising itself as '24-Hour Café – Open 9 to 5'.

For **Dr Loreto Todd** of Leeds University, sourcing the distinctive characteristics of Derry speech is to trace the speaker's origins:

There are quite a number of Ulster Scots people in the Derry area, and you might recognise that by features like '*Oh you canna do that*' and '*you'll no do that*', something that can sound fairly quintessentially Scottish. And of course you get things anyone who's a student of Shakespeare would recognise as an English influence, this love of double superlatives. I heard this relatively recently in the Derry area – I was looking at a house and somebody said to me, 'It's the most deceivingest house you've ever seen' – in other words it looks terribly small but it's terribly big. That sort of feature is very much part of seventeenth-century English and still found in parts of England. Or the double or triple negatives like 'he never said nothing to nobody', 'he never done nothing to nobody' – that sort of feature is very much a part of, if you like, the English tradition.

But if with a very keen ear and a very conscientious approach it is possible for professional linguists like Dr Loreto Todd and Kevin McCafferty to detect and source a few particular features of Derry speech, for the most part it is a rich soup of language which is supped equally by Catholic and Protestant alike. And as **Dr Todd** perceptively points out, language flows and merges and spills over from one part of the region to another, from one side of the border to the other, from one community to another.

People will tend not to distinguish one word from another – why should they? They're not thinking: am I using an English word? Am I using an Irish word? Am I using an Ulster Scots word? Language is simply a medium for them, something that allows them to communicate.

4

CORNWALL

Cornwall is a secretive place. It is a land of deep sea inlets and folded valleys with streams and shaded hollows. The deep-cut Cornish roads are like open-topped tunnels, with views to either side hidden by hedges that tower maybe twelve feet above the roadway.

Old pits driven far into the granite mark where, until a handful of years ago, Cornishmen still blasted and hewed tin out of the earth. Other scars carve out the great white indentations of china-clay pits. And Cornish folk are very private too, folding away the riches of their angular, crusty speech from the ears of outsiders.

Cornwall is a Celtic land, where six hundred years ago the ancient language Kernowek was the national tongue. Then slowly it retreated westwards. It fell into disuse with the spread of powerful and advantageous English as the *lingua franca*, or, as some who resent the cultural burden of a subject-people would say, by the 'sword of the English'.

The study of Cornish talk is secretive too, and surprisingly hard to uncover. The *Survey of English Dialects* pays scant heed to life to the west of the *Tamar*, the county boundary with Devon, and the evidence provided is so thin that Cornish experts regard its sketchy accounts of the presence of Celtic words in Cornish dialect as suspect, if not wholly wrong.

Perhaps Harold Orton and his survey team encountered the same difficulties as we did on *The Routes of English*, when we started looking for locals to sing the glories of Cornish talk. Few were happy and willing to co-operate, preferring to keep their language to themselves.

Why was soon evident. Les Lean, a thoughtful, wry Cornishman, remembered the

The Celts

There is some uncertainty about where the Celtic race originated. Some people say that they came originally from Asia and swept into Europe, driving the European tribes to the extreme edges of the continent and taking up their own position in West Central Europe, around the area of the Danube. The first real signs of their influence in Europe and their culture date from about 800 BC and suggest a hierarchical society ruled by powerful princes and organised in clans. They are reputed to have been warlike but also hospitable, to have been artistic and skillful at making things and to have had a rich oral culture. Their skill in managing the land and in making tools made them wealthy and their fighting skills made them feared by neighbouring tribes.

Gradually they extended their territory. By the 5th century BC they dominated the British isles, assimilating and absorbing the existing natives into their culture. There were two distinct strands of the Celtic culture and of the language. The Goedelic group who spoke Gaelic were dominant in Ireland, the Highlands and Islands of Scotland and the Isle of Man. The other group who occupied the rest of Britain from the Lowlands of Scotland southwards, spoke Brythonic probably up until about the beginning of the 5th century AD. Then, when the Romans withdrew from Britain and groups of Germanic peoples began to arrive from the Danish peninsula in the north and from Germany in the south, a different culture and language began to be established which became known as Anglo-Saxon. The Brythonic language was driven westwards towards Wales and Cornwall and also Cumbria.

When this happened the Cornish and Welsh languages began to diverge and to develop in different ways although there are still similarities. The Cornish language developed from the dialect of Brythonic which was spoken in the south-western part of Britain, as did the Breton language which developed from the language originally spoken by the Cornish people who fled to Brittany in the 5th century. Breton, which is still spoken by a significant number of people in Brittany today, is all that remains of that particular strand of the Celtic language.

mockery he encountered when he and other young men from all over the country found themselves bunked up together doing their National Service. He has been a clay worker all his life, and grew up in tough circumstances near St Austell. The talk he learned in the railway carriage, that was a snug childhood home to him and his family, was pure mid-Cornish. You can ply him with words from the standard Cornish dialect dictionary and he readily identifies them, many of which he still uses freely in his conversation. Whereas for Cumbrians, like Tommy Miller, talking local was a way of keeping things private when you were living cheek-by-jowl with other servicemen, for **Les** it was an embarrassment:

When I went in my National Service in the army they used to laugh every time you'd say things; and then you'd get ribbed and you didn't say 'em, you know. You stopped saying it like. When I used to say that I was 'sweating rivers' and things like that, they would laugh, of course; any word they would... Or they'd laugh at 'r's and things like that. Far from feeling proud of the way you spoke, you felt a bit stupid.

That laughter, that pillorying of the 'ooh-arr' far West Country tones still rankles, and though he is proud of the way he speaks, and of his performances in the local choir and of his work in the church, Les still feels those taunts – you can sense the resentment even now forty years on. In fact even in his beloved male-voice choir, the choirmaster did his best to purge the singers of their Cornish accent:

They'd knock all the 'r's off and things like that. I've had music with the word '*darkness*' in and they crossed out at the 'a' and the 'r' and put '*oc*', '*dock*'. Like it was '*dockness*'. You ain't' supposed to say 'r', you know, in the music, just the 'o'. Leave that out!

After talking to Les, we travelled to Penair School, Truro, thirty or so miles further down the peninsula, heading westwards. As we arrived, the babble of teenaged voices collided with the ringing of bells marking lessons. Yet where were the Cornish accents here? A group of articulate mid-teens looked away embarrassed when the talk turned to dialect, with sniggers about it sounding silly or country-bumpkin-like. These young people could almost have come from anywhere in the south of England, judging purely from the way they speak. Theirs were the flattened-out vowels and rounded off consonants of the Thames Valley, with a faint echo of a voiced 'r' or a pinched vowel that showed evidence of where they had been born. There are few more persuasive playground pressures than the ridicule of your peers, and if, for these young Truronians, to talk local means to be laughed at, they are going to stop, quick.

And they have. Young people, like the **pupils at Penair School**, are acutely aware of how they sound and how they want to be heard to sound:

Sometimes my mum comes out with words that are quite Cornish and I take the mick. Because it's funny, because most people that live in Cornwall, younger people, they don't

Boscastle Harbour at high tide. The inner
harbour at Boscastle was built by Sir Richard
Grenville in 1584. It was a major port used for
exporting things such as slate and corn and
for receiving food and coal for the people of
Cornwall. The prefix Bos-, meaning 'dwelling'
or 'home' is common in Cornish place names.

speak like that any more. The older people, like my parents and my grandparents, they come out with words that are more Cornish than younger children.

And when I'm with my friends down town or something, just to be funny I go up to them and say 'all right my bird', like that and just muck about and just have a laugh really.

The word 'wash': everyone takes the mick out of me when I say that – not the word, just how I say it, *warsh* 'cos they just don't think it's right, 'cos it's not normal. 'Cos like everyone on TV they all speak English, not Cornish, and everyone's used to English. So if you speak Cornish they just think it's funny and take the mick.

Truro has not got the amenities the young people there would like. They want skate-parks that are not going to cost them all their pocket-money every week. They want a swimming pool that has a wave machine and a flume. In fact, they don't actually want to be here at all. Teenagers are rarely happy with their lot and one should perhaps not read too pessimistic a message for the livelihood of Cornish speech and Cornish spirit from what these young people had to say. Yet there is no doubt that their horizons were broader than the shores of Cornwall; they felt penned in by the long peninsularity of the county and they wanted out, for fun, for cash and for a career.

A short gull's flight down into town from the heights of Penair lives Bert Biscoe, local councillor in Truro and a poet who champions Cornwall and its people. His house is perched on the side of the steep hill that rises from the harbour with a view that embraces the quays and the steeply pitched roofs of the town, clustered round the dominant mass of Truro's cathedral. **Bert** is an optimist.

I think Cornish people like their persona; I think they like their humour; I think they like themselves, I think they like to be together. I think that when they are in what you might

call 'mixed' (i.e. non-Cornish) company, they like to rub along with everybody else, they like to make people feel welcome. Part of that I think is to, is to entertain in a quiet way, but part of it is not to put people on edge by making them feel excluded from a conversation. The Cornish do not use their dialect as openly or as aggressively as they might and I would actually encourage people to be more aggressive about it

However, it is hard to imagine how the Cornish, with its mysterious vocabulary, its warm, cottagey turns of phrase and its pronunciation as full of rich crunchy bits as the best Cornish clotted cream, can survive long into the generation of internet-surfing youths and couch-potato TV watchers. Despite what Bert Biscoe may say, they seem to be utterly rejecting their linguistic birthright. However, some may rediscover it, and Nick Darke, a Cornish playwright, talked about the way a local actor has been creating waves of intense interest amongst local schoolchildren with his Cornish theatre workshops where the indigenous talk is strongly encouraged. But the truth is – as the children from Penair School affirm – there are many incomers in Truro (it is after all the county town) and non-Cornish speakers, if not in the majority, are all around them. The norm is changing.

Statistics suggest that as many as half the population of Cornwall comes from beyond the *River Tamar*, lured by the natural beauty of the scenery, the climate and by jobs in the holiday industry. It's not an industry, in fact, claimed Nick Darke, but a trade. Industry, he says, is productive, with something to show for it. Tourism is merely trade. He reckons it is leeching the Cornishness out of Cornwall. And out of the language.

He should know. Born in a beautiful, old stone house at the very edge of the beach near Padstow on Cornwall's north coast, he moved away and knew great success in London

Mine ruins, Caradon Hill, Minions, Bodmin Moor. Tin mining has been an important industry in Cornwall from prehistoric times right up to the twentieth century. The tin produced in Cornwall provided most of the needs of England and Europe until the middle of the nineteenth century when the mines were worked out. By the end of the late nineteenth century there was a greatly increased demand for tin, owing to the development of the tinned food industry and it became necessary to import tin from other countries such as Peru.

and elsewhere with his plays such as *The King of Prussia* and *The Riot*. Now he has returned to live within the sound of the sea, in the house where he was born. It's a house that pays active tribute to the waters that surge up the beach every day, carrying their booty from the high seas. From great baulks of wood, Nick has fashioned shelves and tables; bright orange floats and castaway fishing tackle festoon and decorate the rooms.

Nick's trove is linguistic too. He knows the old Cornish names for every cove and rock along the coast from his home. They are navigational points for when he is out fishing or tending his lobster-pots. Many of the old names have direct Celtic roots going back to times when Kernowek flourished. Today, the folk memory of these old names is ebbing fast. Tourism has pushed the old *slingers* or peripatetic farm workers off the land and the old men and women whom Nick's father used to enjoy tape-recording as they yarned on, forty or so years ago, are all dead. **Nick**:

Pretty well everybody in the parish was associated with agriculture and coupled with the inexorable decline of agriculture has been the inexorable rise of the tourist trade and this has affected this parish very, very strongly. The cost of housing has gone up, the demand for houses on this coastal parish has just rocketed over the last thirty, forty years. So a property anywhere in this parish is way beyond what anybody who works, lives and works locally can afford. If you own a house, you get more money by renting it out in the summer and keeping it empty in the winter than by renting it all the year round. Now the local people, the children of the local people, particularly the farming people, who can't get work on the farms, have had to move inland, further and further inland in order to be able to find somewhere to live.

Cornish Place Names

There is an old saying:
'By Tre, Lan, Ros, Car Pol or Pen'
Ye shall know most Cornishmen'

People with surnames beginning in this way have got their names from places, and in Cornwall many place names begin with these Celtic prefixes.

TRE – which is pronounced 'tray' originally meant a farming settlement but later on it came to mean village or farming community. It is often followed by a person's name, probably the name of the settlement's founder or a prominent person when the community was first established. E.g. Trevarrick, Trewithian, Trevisco and others.

LAN – means a church enclosure and usually indicates that this was an early Christian foundation of the Celtic church. This would be within a round or oval earthwork, often re-using a prehistoric earthwork. E.g. Lanlivet, Lanreath and Lansallos.

ROS or ROSE – originally meant a promontory and then came to be used more often to mean a

And the people who have moved in are the people with a little bit more money who could sell their house for more money in the Midlands, or in London, or the South-East, or wherever they came from. Then they would come to Cornwall, buy a house for a little bit less, but for more than the local Cornish people could afford, they'd move in and then they'd make a living either out of building, or out of the tourist trade.

That has all kinds of implications, particularly with the dialect and the language, because every rock and every cove on this coastline has a name. And it's a name given to it by the old Cornish people. And the reason that they all have a name is because they were all used for one reason or another. You gave something a name because it needed to have a name. And now those names are disappearing because nobody needs to know the names today.

You don't even need to know the name when somebody falls off the cliff into one of the coves. You've got a latitude and a longitude and a satellite navigation number that you can give it, so even the Coastguard doesn't know the names of the rocks and the coves anymore.

I can quote you every single name from Porth Mear, Butter Cove, Higher Butter Cove, Lower Butter Cove, Totty Cove, Rubble Cove, High Cove, Turtle Rock, Porth and Gair, Mackerel Cove, Pentire Steps, Redcliff Castle, Red Cove, along here Rowan Minnows, Fox Cove, Wine Cove, Warren Cove, the Chick, Trescore Islands and Jan Leverton's Island, Arch Rock, Will's Rock, Horse Pools, Saint Merryn Long Cove, St Eval Long Cove – every one's got a name. The list is endless and that's all just within half a mile of where we're sitting now.

slope going down to the sea. Then because these sorts of slopes were not able to be cultivated, but remained rough the prefix ros- often came to mean simply heathland. E.g. Rosemullion Head, Roskorwell and Rosevean.

CAR – this suggests an enclosed settlement whose site provides a good defence against possible enemies. It was a farming settlement but also a fort. It sometimes takes the form GEAR or CAER (similar to the Welsh word) and may be related to the Latin word *Castrum*. It is not the same as the word CARN which means rock formation or crag, although both words suggest height and defensive position. E.g. Carharrack, Carnkiel or Carnyorth.

POL (sometimes appears as POLL, both pronounced pole) – originally meant a pool or a pit and then later came to be used to describe a cove, although PORTH is a more usual way of describing a cove, particularly one where a boat can be landed. E.g. Polzeath, Polperro and Porthleven around the coast of Cornwall.

PEN – usually means headland as in Penzance, but it sometimes also means end or top or principal. It may have come originally from an Old Cornish word ben meaning the foot or end.

Not only do today's locals no longer need to know the traditional names for the features that dot the coast on the Ordnance Survey map, the tourist trade is driving the old names forcibly away, renaming old coves with reach-me-down, off-the-shelf names that owe nothing to the linguistic heritage of Cornwall and everything to Hollywood and a Disneyfied imported culture. **Nick** continued:

Like Trescore River, which isn't a river at all; it's a channel between the three rocks and the cliff, but at low water when the tide's coming in it behaves like a river, it flows like a river, which is why it's called a river. And the old men would shoot trammel nets across that for bass and for flat fish, for sole. And they would call it 'the river' because it behaved like a river. Now it's called by the visitors 'the Blue Lagoon', which I hate. And there's Round Hole which is where the rock formation has collapsed and there's a round hole that you can walk through. That's called 'the Witches Cave' or something. And that to me is a kind of second rate naming of coves.

Even if tourism is supplanting the old names and the people who need to know them, and even if Cornish youngsters feel self-conscious about sounding too Cornish, open an Ordnance Survey map of the county and the rich heritage of the linguistic past is displayed.

Richard Gendall is a Research Fellow at the Institute of Cornish Studies at Exeter University and a former languages teacher, who lives in a magnificent ancient stone house tucked away up a no-through-road in the tiny village of Menheniot, a sprinkle of dwellings on the Ordnance Survey Map, near Liskeard. The map is a very good guide, he says, to the way in which the different influences affected the county in different ways. As the English encroached, bearing their language, the Celtic Cornish language generally retreated westwards.

The Cornish language fell back westwards from the *Tamar* over a period of about eight hundred years and English came in from the east. So English (in the form of the Wessex dialect) gradually encroached over the *Tamar* and moved further west. In the east of Cornwall you get a preponderance of Wessex words, many of them are Middle English or Old English words. In the west you get more Celtic words coming in. And in mid-Cornwall you get a mixture of the two. You can go by the spelling of place names quite often. I mean the area where we live, in Menheniot, was a pocket of resistance to the English. You find place name spellings in this area which match the Celtic west. But it rather seems to indicate that there was a sort of 'slow fade' here.

Where travelling was easier, particularly in north Cornwall, where it was very much easier to ride down because the *River Tamar* is much narrower, access was much easier, therefore people from England came in and there's much more English up there than there was down here.

You find a name like Smallacoombe, which might be in Devon – that's sort of Englishy and a sort of West Country name.

And then at what we call 'Lanson' (Launceston) there's a great spearhead of Cornish names, which have just stayed there and haven't been obliterated. And then you get to Bodmin Moor, which was more or less uninhabited in the old days, and you get a lot of Middle English names. You get places like Bradford there (which only means 'broad ford'), that's a Middle English name. And then you go west of that and you're getting into an area where there's almost completely Cornish names. So there is an untidy westward movement.

The Lord's Prayer in Cornish

The Cornish language as spoken in the Medieval period had a very complicated grammar with an elaborate system of inflected verbs. By the middle of the eighteenth century, when it was dying out, it had become much simpler. As can be seen from this Cornish version of the Lord's prayer, it had been influenced both by the grammar and the vocabulary of the Anglo-Saxon language from which Modern English is principally derived.

Agon Taze nye, eze en Neve	Our Father, which art in Heaven
Benegas bo tha Hanow.	Hallowed be thy name
Tha Gwalaskath gwrenz doaz;	Thy Kingdom come
Tha Voth bo gwreze	They Will be done
En Noer pecarra en Neve.	On Earth as it is in Heaven
Ro tha nye an journama gon bara pub death,	Give us this day our daily bread,
Ha gave tha nye gon pehasow	And forgive us our trespasses
Pecarra tel era nye gava angye	As we forgive them
Neb eze peha war agon bidn	Who trespass against us.
Ha na raze gon lewa en antall,	And lead us not into temptation,
Buz gweeth nye thurt droeg.	But deliver us from evil.
Rag an Gwlaskath Che a beaw	For Thine is the Kingdom,
Han Neath, han Worrians,	The Power and the Glory
Rag nevra venitha.	For ever and ever.
Andelna ra bo	Amen

The changing face of language within the county can be tracked by official documents and legal permissions.

I think the Cornish language ceased to be spoken here in east Cornwall during the fifteenth century, or by fifteen hundred certainly, because the vicar of Menheniot, John Mormon, actually got permission from the church to teach the Lord's Prayer and commandments and the common prayers in English for the first time. Because normally the rule was that you taught this in the vernacular, that is to say, in Cornish. The fact that he got permission to teach in English probably means that the Cornish had died out. And that's the first recorded official permission to teach these prayers in English. We know that the Bodmin area was still using Cornish round about fifteen hundred. But between fifteen hundred and seventeen hundred it fell right back from Bodmin to west of Truro.

By the eighteenth century, the old Celtic language had retreated to the coastal margins of the western extremities of the peninsula, as attested by the researches of a

Welshman, Dr Edward Clwyd. It was about this time that the very last purely monoglot Cornishman – that is to say the last man speaking exclusively Cornish and no English – died, though people continued for many years with both languages at their command. Folklore has it that Cornish was dead by the end of the eighteenth century. In fact, maintains **Richard Gendall**, the dwindling and eventual extinction of Cornish as an actively spoken language (as opposed to today's usage which is, of course, acquired by secondary learning), has been somewhat exaggerated. The evidence, he says, comes from a retired policeman called Botherris who was researching as late as the closing years of the nineteenth century.

This ex-policeman, Botherris, said that as a young man in about 1875 he went to sea with fishermen who spoke Cornish when they were at sea. And this is similarly semi-corroborated by the fact that in the fishing areas quite a lot of fishing words survived. And in St Ives, in my lifetime, in the 1920s and 1930s when they launched the boats over the beach, a man used to stand on the quay wearing a bowler hat and shout out *hunshy berey.* And that means 'heave away now!'. And that is, as far as I know, the last recorded sentence from the language ever used. And that's very late.

But if Cornish today only survives thanks to enthusiasts who learn it from books, much more of it survived either intact or in macaronic form locked into the Cornish variety of English. **Richard Gendall** observes that in the labour-intensive local industries – fishing, farming and mining – before the advent of machinery, conversation flourished and men would readily pass the vocabulary on from one generation to the next.

But as we have observed elsewhere in this book, as the need for the old local term waned with the arrival of new machinery or the supplanting of the industry itself, so the old words were abandoned. However, there is much old Cornish still firmly embedded in the English spoken in the county, and – as we mentioned earlier in this chapter – far more than the thirty or so terms the *Survey of English Dialects* threw up in the late 1950s. **Richard Gendall and his wife Jan** are quick to pick up examples of Cornish that they hear dropped casually into conversation. Maybe the instances are not widespread, and certainly not preponderant, but they have lit upon countless examples in their beachcombing of the conversations they hear in their day-to-day business, or in connection with a programme they host on BBC Radio Cornwall.

There are hundreds. And many have been overlooked that I'm painfully aware are going to be lost. There are certainly Cornish words being used this day, which have come from the old Celtic language, that nobody knows are there.

I mean there's *skudma* for example, that is still in use down west. I've got a recording of an old man talking about going around the beach picking up *skudma* – bits and pieces of jetsom on the beach – and that is straight from the language.

When I was interviewing two elderly people down in Sennen Cove, a lady suddenly came out with the expression 'stacked up like a *golighty*'. We asked her what she meant by *golighty* and she said 'a lighthouse'. And that's almost identical to the Welsh word *golidy*, which means a lighthouse. But this word had never been recorded in old Cornish, and yet it was in use amongst the common people all the time. It literally means light – *golo*, *ty* – house.

Since then with the programmes that we do with the BBC, in the last two years we've come across several 'new' old words, like *shiak*, which means 'untidy'. Never heard of it before. I found it in the Breton dictionary as S-I-E-K, *siek* And it just means 'ready for tidying', in effect 'to tidy up'. And things like this are coming out all the time.

One of the features of Cornish dialect is its variability. The fact that the county is a long, narrow peninsula means that the distribution of certain local terms varies from west to east. And so marked are the differences that, even today when communications are instantaneous and constant, an east Cornishman may be completely unaware of the equivalent term from the other end of the county. **Jan Gendall**, speaking in Menheniot in the east, explained:

If you take a lunch out to a field up this end of Cornwall, you'd say you were carrying your *crib* out to the field, or having your *crib* at work. Down west that's *croust*. If you go into the middle of Cornwall they're more precise and the *crib* is eaten in the morning, the eleven o'clock break, and the *croust* is the afternoon break. Then there are words like *grammersow* and *sow pig*, meaning 'wood lice', and there are many different names for these where the difference between east and west is so great that if you use the wrong name in the wrong area they wouldn't know what you were talking about.

Les Lean spoke about his working life in one of Cornwall's enduring industries, china clay extraction near St Austell. *The clay* – like fishing and the now extinguished tin-mining – is a closed world where local language and jargon can flourish unimpeded. In his young days he was a *kettle-boy* and this being in central/east Cornwall, it was the men's *crib*, or packed-lunch, that it was his job to prepare, ready for their break in the *crib-hut*. Invariably, this consisted of a pasty, and woe betide the kettle-boy who got them mixed up!

I used to know all the pasties, all the makes of all the men's pasties, different types of them. All different shapes, different crimping on the top, used to know 'em all. Some of the men would start work early, then I'd have to warm their pasties up and then the others come in at seven o'clock. They'd probably have their *crib* at ten. Something like that. And then some would rather have it at dinner time. Sometimes if I didn't get 'em hot or get

'em ready, and the fire weren't going right, they didn't like it very much, and they'd get *teasy* on me – 'get mad' – *teasy* [pronounced 'tea-sea'].

We had different words we used to use that we don't now, you know. For instance when they said 'cry' now, we used to say *squall*. Say my sister used to have a daughter that was crying a lot she'd say, 'if you don't stop crying, I'll give you something to *squall* for'. *Squalling*. And moles in the fields we used to call *wants* (to rhyme with 'pants'). *Want-heaps. Wants.* And when we used to say someone was going around with her tail up in the air we would say 'they *got the wap*' (to be over-excited). And I used to go up top of the downs where I used to live and we picked some *urts* and went home and had an *urt tart*. It's blueberries or something like that, I suppose ... I only know 'em as *urts*.

Les Lean and another inveterate local language-collector **Frank Sutton** both pay tribute to the work of the late Ken Phillipps. *The Glossary of the Cornish Dialect*, published in 1993 by this long-time student of local Cornish talk lists hundreds of words that are or have been in common currency. Through his local radio programme, which, like that of the Gendalls now, was hugely important in keeping alive and anthologising the riches of Cornish talk, he gathered the most comprehensive list of words and their meanings to be published in recent years.

Under 'S' you find the innocent-sounding *some,* which has in Cornish the very specific meaning of 'very'. **Frank Sutton**:

There'd be an expression – a couple of old gents sitting on the seat and a young lady would walk by and one would say, *Some 'andsome maid* – a very handsome girl.

To which **Les Lean** responds:

I always call my sisters *maid* now, always refer to *maid.* I always say to 'em: 'all right, *maid'* [pronounced with a short 'e', 'mehd'].

Some handsome, maid – the local usages tumble out from Frank and Les effortlessly – like a couple of other favourites, *fitty* and *maze.* **Les**:

Well *maze, mazed* – it means something similar to *teasy.* Oh, I got mad, you know, I've been *maze.* To get maze, some maze (very angry). *Some maze, get maze.*

Frank: It's a corruption of the English 'amazed'. A lot of the Cornish words in dialect are corruptions of English words.

Les: And *fitty* – *fitty* job. Like you'd say 'he done a good job, real fitty job'.

Frank: *fitty* – it means 'fitting', you see.

For these men, as with many of the older generation of Cornish men and women, the way they speak holds the key to their grip on the place in which they live. It is the Cornish way, despite the ridicule that outsiders at National Service poured upon it. They treasure it and, in albeit a quiet way, trumpet its glories.

But try this list of simple regular and quite normal Cornishisms on the young folk of Penair School in Truro, the county town, and they don't want to know. *Fitty* stirs not a flicker of recognition, and *some handsome* is dismissed as laughably quaint, never to be used. Neither can any of these six fairly representative young people identify the meaning of what I consider a splendidly useful word in normal Cornish speech, a *spence*. No obvious etymological help here for outsiders: a *spence* is what Cornish people call that useful cupboard-under-the-stairs that so often houses brooms, vacuum cleaners and the electricity meter. So now you know.

For these teenagers, the words that trip off the tongue, comfortable, fashionable and stigma-free are virtually the same as the list to be heard amongst youngsters of comparable age in Ashington or Herefordshire or London – *banging, beast, plush* and *pukka, skanky* and *lame*. To get a whiff of the stigma Cornish has to bear amongst these Cornishmen and women of tomorrow, listen to young **Natasha**:

My auntie married this bloke called Al and he is really Cornish, you can't understand a word he says. It's like really bad. It's like when you talk to him you're like sitting there and he's just going ... like this, and it's really Cornish. And it's funny. You don't understand anything they say. Plus on TV and with music, like they all talk... none of them are Cornish. I don't know why they don't, they're not very good at stuff like that. But they're like always on the TV and like people speak like them. And if they're not speaking like them it doesn't seem right...

It doesn't seem right. ... To many older people in Cornwall, what does not seem right is that these young people of Cornwall – and almost all spoke warmly about their county, at least in general terms – should feel that the language is *not* part of being Cornish.

Nick Darke and Bert Biscoe are two ardent spokesmen for the preservation of the Cornishness of Cornwall and its cultural – and in some respects political – independence. Neither is particularly old, but both speak with a very special passion about what is happening to their linguistic inheritance. **Nick Darke** said:

It does cause me great pain because I have a great kind of romantic yearning for my childhood and it was much simpler in those days. So I'm not particularly happy with the way things are now for various different reasons. There was a lot about the old days which could have been preserved and hasn't been. The old people didn't leave it out of their own volition but it was, in a sense, forced out. Almost a kind of very English ethnic cleansing has gone on in this parish and I don't like that very much. But in Cornwall there are many people who very deliberately retain their Cornish and are very proud of their Cornish roots. I do speak to a lot of people like that. And even five miles inland in St Columb it's still a very Cornish town. The change has happened quickly in a very kind of narrow band along the coast line.

More optimistically, **Bert Biscoe** said:

I feel that we're actually making significant progress. I mean if you talk to six young people at Penair School and they say, even somewhat sheepishly, that they are Cornish then I consider that we've made progress. If you asked them that question five years ago I think they would have said something different.

But there are many pressures on them: the *Western Morning News* may carry a survey saying something like 'people with Cornish accents are the least sexy people in the world', and it just ends up becoming a pressure. And you get people who say 'you've got to talk proper'. But what does it matter as long as you're comprehensible?

The problem is that, as the result of these pressures, many of the young – and not so young – people now feel very self-conscious about themselves. I think that self-consciousness has contributed to this kind of self-effacement I've spoken about. We need to actually get ourselves back into the mind set where we value ourselves for what we are and for the way we want to live. And now I feel that I'm part of a people who are actually looking avidly for a future.

Part of that future is to ignite a contemporary Cornish dialect, you know which involves 'surfology', involves rock and 'rock-ology' – whatever we have to deal with. But underpinning it all I always find that no matter what jargon you're talking to a Cornish person in, behind it there's always that sense of irony, of dryness, of using a metaphor from the small world to describe the cosmic.

The Cornish character, I think, is something which Cornish people are beginning again to have a great deal more confidence in, and talking to young people, they actually find something attractive in it, which will sustain them.

5

BRIXTON

Previous page: Brixton High Street. There are few sections of modern youth more lifestyle conscious than the Afro-Caribbean. Much of the language of many young groups when talking about their life, their music, clothes, clubs and the like comes from the Caribbean. Nowhere more so than in the multi-ethnic neighbourhood of Brixton.

Right: Fish as varied and colourful as the customers of the fishmonger.

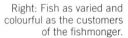

'Wicked!'; 'Bad'; 'Rare'...across the country a new language of appreciation and approbation is widely adopted in schoolyard and danceclub alike. Young people have, as ever, their own hot talk, a utilitarian language of discourse that works. And it works in a number of ways. Of all the microdialects of Britain at the start of the twenty-first century, this language of youth is the fastest moving and the most shaped by fashion. Most parents have experienced a failed attempt at tuning in to the language of teenage offspring, rebuffed by the indignant youngster with ridicule at the wrong word used at the wrong time: 'Oh no, that's old! Nobody says that any more'.

As we saw in Cornwall and in Northumberland, there appears to be growing in Britain a new 'horizontal' form of dialect. This is not one determined exclusively by location or profession, but more by age-group and fashion, social aspiration and new national norms of conformity. You can find it, spread by a shared music culture and by television and radio, virtually anywhere in the UK. Sometimes subversive, often secretive, it occasionally breaks cover into the high-profile arena of television comedy, with, for instance, the antics of Ali G and his team. Where does it come from? Much of it – at least the more prominent words – comes from the Caribbean, to produce what is arguably the most vibrant and dynamic language in Britain today. It is essentially the talk of the country's young black population in places like Liverpool, Bristol and London.

Brixton. For a generation, the name Brixton was a symbol of multicultural community life – and sometimes for disharmony. The residential area of south London, became a

England meets Bengal meets Trinidad meets Poland meets etc.

shorthand for violent and fiery conflict that for many marked the lowest points of Margaret Thatcher's premiership. There was a rash of inner-city flashpoints – Toxteth in Liverpool, St Paul's in Bristol, Broadwater Farm in Haringey, London. However, it was perhaps the serious disturbances of April 1981 in Brixton that came most directly to mean trouble, racial trouble, stand-offs between black rioters and white police with shields and water-cannon, pitched battles, burned out buildings and fervent appeals for calm from community leaders.

That is now in the past and twenty years of evolution in British society has done much to heal some of the worst divisions. Emerging on a warm overcast autumn afternoon from the shiny portal of the refurbished Brixton tube station, one is greeted by the sweet scent of spices and the sharp, briny smells of the fresh fish and grocery shops of Atlantic Road and Electric Avenue. The tangle of streets twist through the railway arches carrying intersecting lines in and out of Brixton's underground and overground stations. On the pavements, the crowds are as diverse a lot as you find in any inner London borough. It is a palette of blacks, browns, yellows and whites, and a soundscape of laughter and cross-rhythmical beats – a picture of multicultural diversity.

Head off down Railton Road towards Herne Hill and there is not a sign of the furious bloody clashes of 1981 when it was the centre of the rioting that put Brixton in the headlines and Railton Road into the list of places with a 'past'. This suburban avenue, long and lined with trimly kept two-storey terraces, runs south from the railway.

Melvyn Bragg came to Railton Road to find the heart of the black linguistic culture. This culture is fashionable today, yet its past is tangled with the painful history of black and white relations over four hundred years – from slavery and colonisation, to the racism which greeted the immigrants arriving in Britain aboard the *Windrush* in 1948.

The Hamilton Arms on Railton Road is like many a 'local' across the country, with its slightly gloomy saloon and TV playing at full blast. It was here that Melvyn Bragg met the acclaimed 'father of Dub poetry', **Linton Kwesi Johnson**.

Being a poet, his business is language. His ear is fine-tuned for the richness of rhyme and assonance and rhythm that runs naturally through the language of the people round here, and which forms the pulse of the language he uses in his writing. He has noticed this local language grow, as one generation of black Londoners has been followed by the next.

The black community here from the Caribbean brought their languages with them, the various islands' dialects. And what I've noticed with some of my children's generation is that they've evolved a new kind of 'black English', if you like, which has Jamaican roots but is different from what my generation speaks. I'll give you some examples – for instance, there's a dance – a rather intimate dance – we do to reggae music, between man and woman, that we call that the *scrub*. The black kids over here say *crub*, and they leave off the 's'. Then again, 'go on' in Jamaican would be *gwan*. But the black kids over here say *gwanin*, which I find really quaint – *gwanin*. So yes, if we've had a Jamaicanisation of the English language in Jamaica; we're now getting a Londonisation if you like, and it's like a second stage of transformation of the language.

From the working mens' clubs of the
North-East to the friendly pubs of
Brixton our team went out and about in
the field to examine the roots of English.
It's a tough job, but someone has to do
it. Simon 'the sound' catches the banter
of Melvyn Bragg and Linton Kwesi
Johnson in the Hamilton Arms, Brixton.

Evolution, transformation. As we have seen throughout the story of the unrolling of the routes of English, the language has been subject to constant change, mutating and absorbing to accommodate new requirements, new fashions, new acquisitions. Caribbean English, and its seedlings that took root in Britain, are flourishing as never before. Caribbean English is a language born of transformation and change more than most others. In order to understand where this language , which occurs throughout so much of urban Britain, comes from, you have to understand the complex and often tortured history of language in the Caribbean. At the beginning, Caribbean English was a way of communicating in its most central, its purest sense. It sprang from the need for different African slave peoples to be able to speak to one another.

But there is more, because in terms of the thousand-year cycle that *The Routes of English* series encompasses, that is a relatively recent evolution. Before the slaves' transportation to the islands, the indigenous languages had been a variety of Amerindian tongues. **Gertrude Buscher**, until recently, Reader in English Language at the University of Hull, has made a special study of the history of the speech of the Caribbean; she explained:

We don't know exactly, but a thousand years ago the islands almost certainly would have had an Amerindian language of some kind, and in Jamaica that was probably Tinil, which is an Arawakan language. That certainly was the case when Columbus arrived at the end of the fifteenth century. In the eastern Caribbean there probably would have been an Arawakan language and Carib. They are languages which mostly have disappeared, but they are still alive in the sense that they've given us some words that we actually use in English, such as 'iguana' and 'papaya'.

But these vestiges are a paltry heritage for a people wiped out by colonising Europeans. We know that Christopher Columbus arrived at Jamaica on his third voyage and that the wholesale slaughter of the indigenous Arawak people meant that a hundred years later none remained. Archaeologists now reckon there were several different Indian peoples and cultures scattered throughout the islands of the Caribbean, as **Jim Walvin**, who is Professor of History at York University, told Melvyn Bragg:

It's always said that the Spaniards first of all fell on their knees and then fell upon the Indians and very quickly the native peoples died out. Until very recently we didn't know very much about them, but archaeologists have now found some extraordinary artefacts about the cultures and the movements of Caribbean peoples between the islands. However, by the end of the eighteenth century they disappeared almost totally, and there are very few left now.

So the native languages were virtually rendered extinct. As Spanish conquerors were supplanted by the British – Cromwell's expeditionary force took Jamaica in 1655, for example – almost all linguistic trace of the Spanish occupation vanished. But it was the era of slavery that brought Caribbean English into being. It was the infamous trade in human beings, when men's lives and livelihoods were seen as commodities to be bought and sold, before the notion of the rights of man had taken root, which made it a necessary. We have seen earlier in *The Routes of English* the way in which trade in goods – buying and selling, trading, bargaining, exchanging – has brought about profound linguistic change. But this trade in men required special linguistic skills. Because neither the people being traded – nor those trading them – had a common tongue. Compromise was required; some form of communication in which question and answer, proposal and counter-proposal could be reconciled and understood. When some form of rudimentary language of barter, of trade develops between peoples who have no shared formal tongue, it is called by linguists a 'pidgin'. The defining characteristic of pidgins is that they are not the native language of anyone – in other words for all their speakers, they are a second or an additional language.

Gertrude Buscher:

What happened is that probably – and quite a lot of this is simply hypothesis – the pidgin stage goes back to Africa when the slaves were transported from Africa to the West Indies. The traders and the slaves didn't share a language and the slaves normally didn't share a language between them either because they were taken from different parts of Africa and therefore wouldn't necessarily be able to talk to each other. And it's quite likely that a kind of pidgin, probably a Portuguese trading pidgin, was spoken on the west coast of Africa. That was the language that was probably used between traders and the people they bought the slaves from. Once the slaves arrived in the Caribbean they would be faced with European masters – in the case of the British colonies, that would have been Englishmen, Scots, and so on. And the working language of the state would obviously have to be something that the overseers and owners could also understand, so that there was contact between native speakers of an African language and native speakers of a form of English.

'Pidgin English' is one of those phrases with which many people are vaguely familiar and which is usually relegated to the curiosities department when language comes up for discussion. But to linguists, pidgins are a fascinating and very precise form of communication.

The prosperity of many of Britain's ports was based not just on 'legitimate' commodities but very largely on the slave trade. The hapless slaves were carried in cramped conditions in slave ships, commonly called coffin ships as they carried the sick, dead and dying slaves often in appalling conditions. The layout of such a ship is shown here.

In the hierarchy of these contact languages, where communication is initially imperfect, the next stage of development is called a Creole. **Gertrude Buscher** draws the distinction:

In the case of a pidgin, what we're talking about is a contact language which is used for a very specific purpose, for trading or in a particular sort of context in which the participants each have their native language, but use the pidgin to carry out whatever function they have to carry out, at a particular time. So that when they've finished they go home and speak their own native language. Whereas a Creole is a language which again arises out of contact (and a lot of people think that the Creoles derive from pidgins), but a Creole is a contact language which has become somebody's native language. Creoles, in fact, are sometimes defined as a 'nativised pidgin'.

This development of language is central to an understanding of how Caribbean English languages – that became the normal languages of discourse in the British administered islands – were shaped. They have their own grammar, their own vocabulary and their own intonation patterns and are very far removed from the standard English that was later taught in the schools of the West Indies, which is, essentially, standard British English.

Historian **Jim Walvin** takes up the account:

It's an interesting story really what happens to languages in the Americas under the slave system, because the slave colonies become a kind of crossroads for cultures and, of course, a crossroads for languages. The number of African peoples deposited in the Americas is something like ten million, drawn from a coastal stretch of Africa from Sene-Gambia down to Angola, and deep into the interior, although in fact the great bulk of the Africans in the British colonies came from Ibo-speaking peoples of Nigeria. And

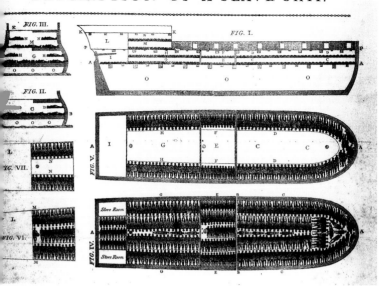

DESCRIPTION OF A SLAVE SHIP.

FIG. III.

FIG. I.

FIG. II.

all of those languages were also mixed, of course, with the major European languages.

Installed in the islands of the Caribbean, the slaves, whose African roots were so diverse as to deprive them of a common *lingua franca*, developed their pidgin – a mix of rudimentary vocabulary and basic grammar – into something far more significant and flexible. Many of them, of course, would become bilingual, speaking both pidgin and a more standard form of the language. **Gertrude Buscher**:

The children born on the estates would probably have heard as a first language a form of speech which was not a 'full language', probably a pidgin. But as they grew up the pidgin would have developed because the child needed to express the whole of its life in a language.

Normally the child wouldn't have been near enough to the speaker of English to have learned English the way a child in England would and therefore the language that children spoke developed in its own kind of way. And the chances are that their vocabulary came very largely from English. But what we don't quite know is exactly how the grammar came about, because the grammar of the Creoles in the West Indies is certainly very different from that of English.

As Jim Walvin has observed, several European languages were in play both in Africa and in the Caribbean, but the influence of English was dominant. This was a very simplified form, but it sowed the seeds. **Mark Sebba,** a lecturer in Linguistics at Lancaster University:

Now this was not nice English, not refined English; it was not something that would be approved of by the makers of grammar books and dictionaries, but it was enough to be able to make rudimentary kinds of communication in the situation in which the slaves found themselves. Despite the fact that the plantation owners were British and English was the ruling language in the cane fields, there was very little contact between English and the Creole. They developed, if you like, in isolation. Really the languages which shaped Creole were African languages much more than English at this time.

But, after the end of slavery, in the first half of the nineteenth century, things did start to ease up a little bit and there was a little bit of social mobility within the colonies and so more of a social continuum developed. People were now able to get a little bit of education and move off the plantations and sometimes take other kinds of work. So instead of the previous polarised linguistic situation, where you had Creole on the one hand and standard English on the other and really nothing in between, you start to find that as people had a bit of access to education they started to learn standard English to some extent.

The pidgins (and later creoles) tended to keep the syntax of the African languages and take on the vocabulary of the European occupiers of the particular island the slaves were shipped to. **Linton Kwesi Johnson**, the great 'dub' poet, confirms the heterogeneous nature of the creoles:

Creole, as I understand it, really is the result of the meeting of different cultures. Take, for example, Caribbean English as we know it. At the core of it is the English language, English words, but it has African, Amerindian, Indic and other European and Chinese influences too, and even though the words may be English, the usage and the meaning is often African.

For example, you get compound words like *hardies*, which means 'stubborn', or *cuteye*, which means giving someone a dirty look. Now those two words 'cut eye' are English, but the actual usage is African. *Kisteet* is another example, you know which is like you go like that [Linton sucks his lips] which is a kind of expression of contempt; and that's very African.

As we have already seen, many words flow into language as a result of commerce, not least through the so-called 'triangular trade' of slaves and sugar with the West Indies. In the early seventeenth century these islands were still a forbidding prospect for settlers and few would venture into the hostile unknown. But at the same time as, for example, the island of St Christopher (later St Kitts) was being colonised – it came under British rule in 1623 – young children were being swept off the streets of London and physically forced to go to the colonies, transported there by the Virginia Company. Some of these were vagrants and were sentenced to transportation by the courts, others were literally 'kidnapped' from the street (which is where the term originated). Their first destination was Virginia, (1607) then Bermuda (1619) and only five years after British rule on the island began, St Kitts saw its first young Londoners transported there in 1628. Barbados, too, saw youngsters sent very early on.

Naturally enough, these young London streetchildren – whose only crime had been to be poor and destitute on the streets of London – carried their talk with them. It is thought that one of the idiosyncratic features of Caribbean creole that has been handed down through generations of speakers and back to London via the West Indians, who came to live in the capital, stems directly from their speech patterns of four hundred years ago. **Dr Laura Wright** of Lucy Cavendish College, Cambridge, a specialist in the evolution of London's English, explains the phenomenon:

One of the things that you can hear in Caribbean English today is a feature where you put a *ye* sound after a 'k' or a 'g' in certain words. So a 'cat' or a 'garden' in many of the Caribbean islands comes out like a *cyat* and *gyarden*. Or if you want to say 'you can't do' something, you would say *I cyan't do it*.

This is something that used to happen in London, but not all Londoners did it – it was a lower-class feature. In 1617 a linguist who signed himself 'Robert Robinson, London' published a book called *The Art of Pronunciation*. In it, he noted that Londoners were beginning to use a 'y' sound in places they hadn't done before. The example he gives is *gyarded* for 'guarded'. Most Londoners would have pronounced their 'r' at this point in time as well so it would have been something more like *gyarrded*, with an 'r' sound.

By 1801 another commentator was praising the sound as 'smooth and elegant'. So by the time you've got through to 1800 it's no longer stigmatised as lower class. 'It distinguishes the polite conversation of London from that of every other part of the island' was the comment.

By the end of the Victorian era it had died out in Southern England but:

You can still hear it to this day in some Irish accents and, of course, you can hear it all over the Caribbean. So when present day Caribbean speakers come and settle in London they're bringing it back again.

Laura Wright identifies a similar phenomenon with the 'w' sound as pronounced by Caribbean English speakers in words where there would be no such sound in standard English.

Today we don't tend to think of 'w's as a particularly significant or salient sound in London speech, but in the Caribbean you can hear people saying things like *bwoy* and *cwome* and *bwoil* for 'boy' and 'come' and 'boil' and even *pwot* for 'pot'. Yet again this was an original London feature: first of all the poor Londoners did it, then the more middle class Londoners, then it became something that was excellent or fashionable to do in London speech. Over it went to the colonies and you can still hear it there nowadays, and if they come back here then you hear it here too.

It is important to stress that the creole forms that we are talking about in the islands are not strictly varieties of English, in the same way as American or Australian English are. They are language systems that use many of the lexical items that English uses, but have developed their own internal coherence. There are many different forms of Caribbean creole English in the West Indies, but for a number of reasons, it is the Jamaican variety that has most strongly taken root in Britain and that has shaped the so-called 'black London' speech that has developed from it. **Gertrude Buscher** examines some of the finer points of how Jamaican creole operates:

For instance, the verb system is quite different from that of English. English expresses the different tenses, for example, by adding an 'ed' or 'd' at the end of a verb – creole doesn't do that. The creole verb system is in some ways much more akin to some West African languages in which the tense is marked less than perhaps the aspect, the way of looking at the action. And what's more, instead of adding endings, there are particles which are used to express tense, or aspects.

So if we take an English expression such as 'he is going', in Jamaica that would be *im a go*, with the 'a' expressing the idea of something 'going on'. In the past tense there is no ending and very often the simple verb form is used. So you might say *Dan run* (done running) which might mean 'ran', because the context is enough to express the idea that we're talking about the past. But there may also be a particle to mark the past if it isn't clear from the context. So that system is quite different from what you would expect if it was simply a development of English.

And that in turn, asserts **Gertrude Buscher**, affects the way in which we should view the language of, for example, Brixton:

There are people who treat Jamaican as a dialect of English, but I think that's a misuse of the word 'dialect' in the sense of a variant form which has grown organically with and out of a language like Yorkshire or Scots. In the case of Jamaican Creole I don't think that's the case, because Jamaican Creole is the result of a much more cataclysmic event, namely the uprooting of African slaves who had to learn English in circumstances which are not those of dialect learners of a language. The language of the youth scene in London is very largely the result of creole, influenced by Rasta language. It's a development of a language which is not of the same origin as English, even if it shares a lot of the vocabulary of English.

One of the features most referred to by linguists when describing the way the different varieties of talk in the Caribbean have over time related to one another is that of the so-called 'language continuum'. This was a sort of 'rainbow shading' which started at one end with 'pure' standard English and which ended at the other with pure creole. Along the line of the continuum, it is maintained, there were different degrees of acuteness which related largely to class. **Mark Sebba:**

Huge, joyful, colourful, noisy, uplifting, controversial, popular –
London's unique Notting Hill carnival.

The creole in its most different form from standard English was associated with the people right at the bottom of the social scale, those who had no access to education and who often lived either in urban poverty or in very rural areas. At the top of the hierarchy was standard English which, as always, was spoken by the élite, by the professionals, and by the wealthy people who had access to education.

And to some extent that is still the situation today. But the great majority of the population speak something which is neither that very pure and old kind of creole, nor is it standard English, but an in-between variety, and there's actually a technical term for this – we call it a 'misalectal variety'.

But that is not to say that a speaker remains shackled indissolubly to his or her own variety. **Ian Diefenthaller,** a writer on Caribbean poetry,is very aware of how flexible the language play along the continuum can be:

In everyday speech and in poetry to a large extent now, people switch quite readily between the two. It's not a necessarily conscious thing. It might be that if you're in polite company, you might make a conscious effort to speak properly, and if you were at the beach, say, you'd make an effort to probably go the other way. You tend to switch between the two ends of the spectrum quite readily.

Back in the Hamilton Arms in Brixton, **Linton Kwesi Johnson**, one of the most powerful voices of black poetry in Britain, recalls extremes of the 'language continuum' in his own past. Just another example, in fact, of that familiar phenomenon of 'code switching'.

As a kid going to school, if you spoke in an English class the way you would speak to your friends in the playground, you'd be chastised for talking bad and not speaking the Queen's English.

I came just before the door was closed on Commonwealth immigration after the 1962 Immigration Act. So there were people still coming in, which meant that the language was being kept alive by newcomers, adding to the language community. The kids, the black kids, I found most of them in my age group who had been here for two or three years still spoke Jamaican, or we'd speak like Jamaicans when we were together in the playground. But we adopted the English – the London English – accent rather quickly, and if we were communicating with teachers or English boys, we would be speaking London English. Yet among ourselves we'd be speaking as we spoke in the Caribbean.

Sometimes, the code-switching would occur not between social groups, but within them – almost like a linguistic ornamentation, an almost musical verbal grace-note.

Another thing also is that I found as a teenager – growing up I became conscious of it – that sometimes we'd be talking among ourselves and would start a sentence in English, and finish it up in Jamaican, or there'd be Jamaican words put in, some comments, somewhere in the middle of the sentence.

One of the principal features of London Caribbean, or more specifically London Jamaican English (also referred to as Black London) is its musicality. Closely related to the spread and great popularity of reggae, and thereby Rastafarianism, there is a natural beat to many of the speech patterns. Listen to Linton Kwesi Johnson read his poem in honour of the late MP for Tottenham, Bernie Grant, and hear how the lines pulse with a natural rhythm, rhyme and assonance. This is no dialect of English. This is a dialect of Caribbean creole. **Linton Kwesi Johnson**:

What attracted me to poetry from when I was a kid was not just the language of poetry, it was the music of poetry. I tend to find a lot of modern English poetry nowadays very flat, very opaque, very dry and I was really attracted to lyrical poetry; I was attracted to poetry

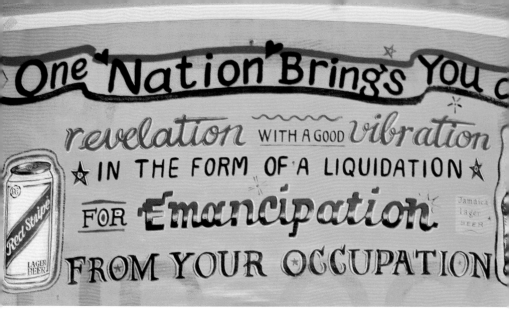

One Nation Brings You
revelation WITH A GOOD vibration
★ IN THE FORM OF A LIQUIDATION ★
FOR Emancipation
FROM YOUR OCCUPATION

that sang. And when I began to write, to find my own poetic voice, I found that music kept on creeping into whatever I wrote. And what I found about the language I was using, was that it lent itself very easily to music. It has musical qualities all of its own. All the inflections of the voice, the tonality, everything. And that's how I compose my music, by simply using the actual structure of the speech to find the rhythm.

Rastafarianism was popularised through reggae music, which became an important source of identity for my generation in particular. And the language of the Rastafarian, just like the Jamaican Creole, was in a sense subverting English grammar. And words like *babylon* for 'the police' became popular, *trud* for 'walk' became popular; the term *dread* and words like those became a part of everyday speech.

There was a need not only to find a way of speaking your identity and pride in that identity loud and clear, but also of reflecting a culture that was sharply different from that of the surrounding – and often openly hostile – British landscape. English – British English – simply wouldn't do as a means of expression; too uptight, too limited, too restrained, too associated with all the negative cultural and historical notions that black Londoners were rejecting. **Ian Diefenthaller** has said:

Edward Kamau Brathwaite, in his *History of the Voice*, explores the development of a suitable language and means of expression that are indigenous to the Anglophone Caribbean – a language suited to the description of West Indian experiences. For example he says, 'A hurricane does not roar in pentameters. What we perceive as English in a poem is not quite English. English it may be, in terms of some of its lexical features, but in its contours, its rhythm, its timbre, its sound explosions, it is not English, even

though the words as you hear them might be English to a greater or lesser degree'.

Brathwaite is looking for a language suitable for describing all the things that West Indian writers want to write about. He wants to use metaphors, he wants to use sounds that illustrate what it is to be West Indian. So his emphasis on the hurricane is the destructive power, the actual feel of the hurricane. It doesn't go with di-dum di-dum di-dum di-dum... He doesn't want the pentameter to dominate his poetry, he wants it to ebb and flow, to rise and fall. He wants to smash up the English and he does this by using the West Indian Creoles.

The detail of how the different layers of locally developing varieties of black English or black British interrelate is the work of much academic study at present. However, it is very hard to pin down with any degree of accuracy or validity, as it is perfectly conceivable that within one year of the publication of this volume many of the terms described could become hopelessly out of date and others will have taken their place. The language is living and growing and new words must be freshly coined for new purposes.

It is constantly subject to change and revision through contact with a fresh influence, a subtlety of fashion, or sudden loss of currency. In certain cases, where a word flows

Linton Kwesi Johnson – the world's first dub poet – was born in Jamaica in 1952. He read the Old Testament psalms to his grandmother and has never forgotten them. He came to London in 1963, swapping green fields for concrete streets of Brixton. Racism put him off education until much later on. In the early 1970s he joined the Black Panther Youth League of the Black Power movement. About this time he began to write poetry seriously, often reciting it in public with a reggae backing. His poetry which was meant to be read out aloud concerns his own experiences of black youth in a largely hostile environment. The reggae rhythms are interwoven with the words.

out of the black community into the mainstream, it can lose its subversive quality and thus its value to the people for whom it was originally most expressive. In this, language (and current British black language in particular) is no different from any micro fashion which when adopted by the mainstream or by a socially 'inappropriate' group immediately becomes unfashionable. (Think of shellsuits, Mexican beer or Tommy Hilfiger leisurewear.)

Perhaps **Tony Thorne**, who is Head of the Language Centre at King's College, University of London, and author of the *Bloomsbury Dictionary of Slang*, knows more than most about the current state of play both in the broad lines of how London black English operates, and in its detail.

It isn't different dialects, it isn't American black, English black, Jamaican black any more, although there are those centres of black language. But the language is swapped and traded and moves between those centres so quickly now that it's often quite hard to tell whether a word originated in black American or black British or black Caribbean, or even black South African. Soweto slang has had a slight influence on this kind of continuum of black language.

Until recently there's been a big difference between the kind of black talk used by an older black generation, using language coming mainly from the Caribbean – patois if you like – and their kids, and younger kids – black and white, who are using a kind of new generation of street slang, which is also black in origin.

But they're very different. So for example the older generation might say the word *vexed*, meaning especially 'furious', 'irritated'. Whereas the younger generation have got lots of other words like *loops, locko, raggo, screwin, buggin, beefin*.... And they would use those words. But the younger people could equally well use *vex*: they would know this word.

So that the younger generation has access, if you like, to that older black English – words like *carn* from 'coin', meaning 'money'; (enough *carn* means 'I've got adequate funds'). This is really older-generation language, but it's been picked up for younger people's street slang as well. Other old-fashioned words that have a new currency are words like *antiman* or *auntieman* for a 'homosexual' - this is old pejorative Jamaican talk, and it's been picked up by a younger generation.

But what I think you're finding now is that the generation gap is breaking down, because you've got older people, parents, now, who are willing to use the same language to some extent as the kids: there's very little difference. They wear the same clothes, they may listen to some of the same music, so you're getting older people using words like *blaf* or *clap* or *raid* meaning 'steal', or *ting*, which is just can be anything. It can be a 'thingummyjig', or it's used about the male member or it's used about drugs, it's almost *anyting* you like.

But to return to the point at which we began this chapter, with the now ubiquitous terms of approbation – and derision – that young people up and down the country seem to have adopted wholesale and which can be sourced, at least indirectly to black British speech. **Tony Thorne** has made a special study of them:

I've looked at the language of particular schools in the same part of London and you'll see quite a big variation from one school to another, and a lot of it is black English, used by black and white kids alike. For example, words for 'good', words for 'excellent' – there are hundreds of them in street talk. One school may say *dark* or *det* or *wicked* or *shuysty* and then the next school will have some of those words but they may also favour the words like *fat* and *tick* and *def* and *chris*, and these are all words which mean 'great', 'excellent', 'ace'. But the particular choice it seems to be partly local, regional, although all the children seem to be aware of the existence of the other terms.

So what, finally, of the means of propagation, of dissemination, of sending these new words into the broader British linguistic arena, such that they gain a wide currency across the country? We have come a very long way from Laura Wright's transported youngsters from 1628 taking their 'y' sounds and their extra 'w's and seeding generations of Caribbean creole with them.

This modern dissemination process can happen overnight. We saw how reggae and its language and rhythms were taken up and spread influence and desirability throughout many parts of the community, reaching out far into white society. Now, with the introduction of Ali G, television has adopted, subverted and popularised a form of self-mocking pseudo-black culture. Since, as we have observed, fashion is fickle, it is possible that within months, Ali G will have been, if not forgotten, then consigned to the archive containing erstwhile Eurovision hits and cabbage-patch dolls. But for a year at the turn of the millennium, Ali G carried the boundaries of language out into new areas. Tony Thorne and, first, Mark Sebba have both observed and studied the phenomenon. **Mark Sebba** comments

Ali G is very interesting because he's a white person pretending to be a black person, but everyone knows that he's a white person pretending to be a black person – he makes the pretence very obvious. And one way that he does that is that on his show he actually has people who are real speakers of creole, who speak creole to him, and then he makes a show of not being able to understand what they're saying to him. And so linguistically, although he uses some of the features which can be associated with people of Caribbean extraction, the way that he does that is really partly intended to show that he is not really a creole speaker himself.

Tony Thorne adds

What's happened, and it's been happening for a long time, is that white kids have imitated black talk. Now black talk's interesting to a linguist because in society in general it is the least prestigious kind of language. It's language of people who still, frankly, don't have much power, economically and socially, and yet on the street, of course, black English is the most privileged, it's the most admired kind of English.

And this is what happens in the playground. Even in schools where there are no black kids you'll find white and Asian kids using this black slang. But this is why someone like Ali G, apart from being very funny, is actually a very, very accurate picture of the kind of wannabe, the 'rude boy', the Asian kid who really identifies with black street culture, even if they actually make themselves a bit ridiculous by doing so.

Thus we end this chapter with one of the paradoxes of contemporary Britain. As Tony Thorne observes, those who have least in material terms and in terms of power possess linguistically what is most prized – amongst young people at any rate. Whether it is a Linton Kwesi Johnson poem that they hold up for emulation, or something more fickle, something more dependent on promotion and visibility, they will effect the way we shall all be talking in the future.

6

OSWESTRY

Previous page: Offa's Dyke. Originally a mound and ditch fortification built by King Offa who ruled the English kingdom of Mercia at the end of the eighth century. It was to mark out the boundary between his country and Wales and to discourage invaders. It has remained, in effect, the boundary between England and Wales ever since.

Right: Not until 1535 was it finally decided, after many battles, that Oswestry was an English town as opposed to Welsh.

AE Housman's poem *A Shropshire Lad* epitomises the spirit of rural England for many people. Tucked south of Cheshire, sandwiched between Staffordshire to the east, and the Welsh border, Shropshire, with its rolling hills and small towns and villages is sometimes described as the 'secret treasure' of England's countryside. Lying at the western extreme of the county is the old market town of Oswestry. This is frontier country, the heart of the Welsh Marches, whose very name means 'boundary'.

Oswestry is a comfortable, snug little town, a jumble of two storey shop fronts – Sayers the Bakers, Pritchards the Gentlemen's Outfitters – lining a tangle of streets that are constantly clogged with cars. Many of the old shops snaking up Church Street, Willow Street, Cross Street and the curiously named Leg Street are disfigured these days, with the unsurprising logos of national chains. Only a few eighteenth and nineteenth century gables and some occasional half-timbering break up the rooflines.

On a Wednesday these Oswestry pavements are filled with bustle. Wednesday is market day and in the pedestrianised streets round the Powys Covered Market, the usual range of plants and pot scourers, meat and many veg are pored over by a mainly middle aged and female tide of customers. Their husbands, meanwhile, are hard at work at the other market in town, the weekly livestock market for sheep and cattle. In Powys Covered Market, the voices are all English; maybe here and there the occasional lilt that suggests Welsh parentage, but for the most part, the accents are Shropshire – 'r's (much like a west-countryman's) clearly audible – mixed with the south-eastern whine of incomers.

Market Day in Oswestry is both a commercial and social event.

Cut to the western fringe of Oswestry and the buzz of conversation round the sheep pens is more mixed. Lots of rich Shropshire, certainly, but many of the earnest discussions about the beasts on offer are in Welsh. The faces, too, are Welsh and, if you ask their names, you find the Williamses and the Pughs and the Powells are ubiquitous. The Welshness of Oswestry Livestock Market is the result of its success. Hill farmers from Wales bring their sheep for sale across the border to Oswestry because they get decent prices here.

If you ask David Ellis, Chairman of the Oswestry branch of the National Farmers' Union, about the nationality of his members, he will tell you that two-thirds are Welsh. However the proceedings of his meetings are all conducted in English. And former leader of Oswestry Council, Beryl Tomley, confirms that, although at least two of her councillors were Welsh-speaking, no-one was ever heard to speak Welsh, even in informal conversations after meetings.

But why should this come as a surprise? After all, Oswestry is in England. Now.

For a long time, this was fought over territory, land that has see-sawed between Welsh and English possession, and while we were visiting, many locals explained, only half-jokingly, that Oswestry was still Welsh. In the damp gloom of an October evening, the local boys of Oswestry Town Youth Football Club gather for practice, unaware, no doubt, of those lines from Housman's *Shropshire Lad* that could have been written with the moment in mind:

'Ay, the ball is flying,
The lads play heart and soul;
The goal stands up, the keeper
Stands up to keep the goal...'

These Shropshire lads cut a dash very different from the romantic ideal of Housman. They were feisty about the Welsh and guyed mercilessly their (English) team-mate Gareth for the Welshness of his name. And **Russell Humphries**, ex-national level boxer and now the team's trainer, was quick to point out that this was still 'combative' territory, especially on a Saturday night.

You get gangs from right next to the Welsh border, because Oswestry's in England; and then you get the boys from Chirk, which is in Wales, who come down – and you're back to the old tribal warfare. Oswestry's renowned for fighting at night, against the Chirk boys and the Wrexham lot. It's gangs from over the border, they come to Oswestry for a bit of fisticuffs. If there's a team of Welsh lads over there on the pitch and my lot started speaking like they do, taking the mick out of the Welsh, there'd have been a battle in the middle of the field.

For a more permanent reminder of this centuries-old rivalry, drive out of town a handful of miles to the west up the Llansilin road and you come to signs for the old race-course. It is the closest spot to Oswestry, where Offa's Dyke, the great earthwork that was thrown up in 784 AD to keep the Welsh out of England, is to be found. To the west lies a rolling line of hills, to the east, the flatter English plains of Shropshire. The divisions here are geographical, topographical, historical – and linguistic. Standing near Offa's Dyke with the divided landscape on either side of him, Melvyn Bragg asked **Dr Robert Penhallurick**, Lecturer in English Language at the University of Wales in

Offa's Dyke

Offa was a powerful king of Mercia in the eighth century AD when England was divided into several states, each with its own ruler. Mercia means 'marches' and is the name given to the central part of England which stretched from Lincolnshire to the counties now known as Shropshire and Gloucestershire, and which has a boundary which 'marches' with the borders of Wales.

After the Romans left Britain, England was divided into several individual states, each with its own king. Mercia had the advantage of being an inland territory and was therefore less at risk of invaders from across the sea. It soon became the most powerful state in the country. However, the savage people of Wales posed some threat, so King Offa had a huge ditch dug, a hundred miles in length, from the mouth of the *Wye* to the mouth of the *Dee*, to mark out the boundary between his country and Wales and to discourage invaders. This was known as Offa's Dyke. It is still traceable today and has remained, in effect, the boundary between England and Wales ever since Offa's time.

Swansea, what we could read from the way people in and around Oswestry speak today.

Here, put simply, the way people speak would say whether they feel themselves to be English or Welsh because one of the conflicts here is, or has been, between the English language and the Welsh language over the last thousand years.

It's perhaps not quite as simple as that though for the Welsh people, in that wherever you go in Wales you will find Welsh people who don't speak Welsh. So the other thing to consider is the English-speaking Welsh people – what kind of English they will be speaking and what that says about their identity. Welsh English certainly comes in many varieties, some of them very historical, particularly those varieties that are being spoken in the traditional 'Welsh Marches'.

Then again, within Welsh you have dialectal variation: you have two major kinds of Welsh – northern Welsh and southern Welsh. And you could argue that these days also you've got a new kind of Welsh emerging which is a more educated kind of Welsh, because it's being taught in schools rather than being passed on at home.

Across the country, at the home of the *Survey of English Dialects* in Leeds, Robert Penhallurick's opposite number is **Dr Clive Upton**. Clive has listened closely to the way the languages of these frontier lands have absorbed and been coloured by their neighbours' – and erstwhile enemies' – speech. Just like that fluctuating boundary, mobile for so many centuries, the English they speak in these parts has always been chameleon-like:

It starts off as a West Midland Mercian type of Old English, but the interesting thing there, if one thinks about it topographically, is that the valleys run east–west out of Wales (or into Wales, depending on which way you're going!) and so a number of these market

King Oswald

King Oswald of Northumbria was a particularly good and Christian king who was canonised after his death in 642 and is sometimes known as St Oswald. During his lifetime England was ravaged by fighting between the different states into which the country was divided, some of which were Christian and some heathen. Northumbria was a powerful state in which the new religion of Christianity was well established. Monasteries were set up and missionaries welcomed and supported, and the great Minster at York was built. However, the Christian kings and leaders were constantly threatened by the heathen kings such as King Penda of Mercia, a fierce and single minded warrior who had no time for any new religion and simply wanted to gain as much power as possible. He was exactly the opposite of Oswald who was reputed, at a battle against the heathen at Hexham to have carried the Cross into battle himself and then after digging it into the ground to make an altar, to have spent time praying with his men, almost up to the moment when the enemy set upon them. Not surprisingly, when they won the battle it was thought to be a miracle and Oswald's Cross was revered as having miraculous powers.

Although he led a saintly life, spreading the Christian gospel and travelling many miles with St Aidan in order to spread the word, he could not, in the end, defeat the Mercian forces and he was defeated by Penda at the battle of Maserfield. His body was hacked to pieces by the savage Penda and bits of it were stuck on stakes to rot, but it is said that the hand which he had used so often to bless his people remained white and incorruptible. From then on, he was regarded with reverence as a saint and the town of Maserfield was renamed Oswestry to honour him.

towns in the Welsh Marches are part-Welsh, part-English. And the English certainly influences the speech of Wales, the Welsh form of English spoken in Powys, for example. But by the same token English forms are affected by Welsh. So, for example, in the south of the West Midlands, on the Welsh border, one would expect people to sound their 'r's, to say things like 'farm' and so on. In parts of that area – West Herefordshire, for example – the 'non-rhotic', non-'r'-sounding Welsh influence comes over.

And by the same token, one will find parts of Wales where that 'r' feature is found. So there's a lot of mixing of Welsh and English forms in the English of the area.

Oswestry is truly a place of divided loyalties. Battles were constantly fought over the territory and it was not until 1535 that the town – just five miles from the border – settled in England. The name Oswestry, incidentally, is a corruption of 'Oswald's Tree' commemorating King Oswald, the Christian monarch who was killed by the pagan King Penda in 642 AD and his body hung from a tree.

This land is the heart of that territory which **Dr Penhallurick** just referred to, the 'Welsh Marches'. This is the name for the border between England and Wales and the term 'march' itself is related to an Old English word for border *mearc* [pronounced merch].

The word 'March', as in the Marches of Wales, came into English from French in the thirteenth century – Old French *marche*, meaning 'boundary', 'limit'. It is related to an Old English word, *mearc*, which has become in modern English 'mark', and both of these words are closely related. In a way it's a good example of the ways in which words themselves cross boundaries.

The Marches were the creation of the Norman kings of England who set up the so-called 'Marcher Lordships' along the border. These were in effect relatively independent petty kingdoms which were established to quell the rebellious Welsh uprisings and ruled over by William the Conqueror's most valued supporters. The territories were known by their Latin name *Marchia Wallia* or the Welsh Marches, while the native Welsh lands were 'Wales proper' or *Pura Wallia*. Robert Penhallurick:

The Marches don't only come down the traditional border between England and Wales, but the old Marcher Lordships extended into South Wales, through Glamorgan, through Gower, and down into Pembroke, and the Normans also established fortresses in isolated locations through North Wales. So there's a kind of band of Norman lordships that were established here, near Oswestry. There was a Norman castle built towards the end of the eleventh century, and it was a way of containing the Welsh, and setting up a kind of transition area between Wales and England.

With a history not only of conflict but of constant ebb and flow across a relatively narrow stretch of territory, it is perhaps unsurprising that the two languages of the area, divided though they are both linguistically (Welsh is a Celtic language related to Cornish and Gaelic, not English) and politically, should have interbred. After all, the peoples of this borderland, despite being traditional enemies, have also, over the centuries, known enormous cross-border contact and trade, friendship and even intermarriage.

The sheepmarket at Oswestry is important for Welsh and English farmers. Both languages can be heard but English tends to predominate.

In the early centuries after the Norman Conquest there was a lot of conflict, but also there was a lot of intermingling, and we can see it even today. You'll hear Welsh spoken in Oswestry, you'll hear English spoken in Oswestry. So there's a lot of to and fro – there's always been a lot of to and fro across this apparent frontier. If, however, you look at the old Marcher Lordships as a whole, as a kind of transition zone, running all the way down the edges of Wales into the southern coastland, then in a way that boundary has remained quite stable, as a zone of English influence, and as a zone which has surrounded the Welsh-speaking areas. Of course, English has now spread all the way across Wales, but there are still those Welsh heartlands contained within that border.

Dr Penhallurick reckons that it's a pretty good bet that, a thousand years ago, the ancestors of the men and women thronging the busy streets of Oswestry on market day would have been Welsh-speakers, not English. Personal names seem to have been predominantly Welsh, though the fact that there was a Saxon settlement not so very far away might well have meant, he says, that you could have overheard the occasional phrase of English – or at least of Anglo Saxon.

Today, the tables are turned, and it is the overheard phrase of Welsh that strikes the ear of an English speaker at the livestock market. At nine in the morning in the snackbar where Linda, a resolutely English-speaking assistant, serves up the steaming burgers and full English breakfasts, the talk of the farmers is in English. According to Linda, who now lives in nearby Morda, but attended a Welsh school where she was taught Welsh, there is as much Welsh as English to be heard at market, if not more. 'Though I can't understand it', she adds, 'just the basics'.

Slip away from the steamy atmosphere of the snackbar; worm your way between the barred hurdles that pen the sheep into rectangular enclosures like a giant and crazy

The auctioneers at Oswestry livestock market walk along the gangplanks selling the sheep as they go. Eavesdroppers and outsiders find their language impenetrable.

maze, and do a bit of eavesdropping. In the knots of farmers casting a professional eye over the lots up for auction, the huddled appraisals are all in Welsh, or almost. Yet – another contrast – when the auctioneer gets underway with his ferocious nineteen-to-the-dozen patter selling premium lots of *tups* (rams) the words are only English (though one Welsh-speaking farmer did confide to me that he reckoned you got better prices if you spoke Welsh). This is the irony, and the rather delightful harmony, of this battle scarred land. In farming, these men and women seem to have found a common ground that unites them and the language they use to describe their farming seems to matter less.

There is, however, an overriding sense of regret in the voices of several farmers we spoke to, whose native language was Welsh, but for whom the attractions of the heart had proved too strong. Welsh-speaking man marries monoglot English girl does not sound like much of a tragedy, but the sadness was there 'it's always the way, isn't it?' we heard from the men, with a sigh, 'we speak English at home now'.

According to **Robert Penhallurick**, this is a trend that started nearly a thousand years ago:

The long process of anglicisation began with the Normans, with the Lordships. The Normans established castles and set up the first towns: this is the pattern throughout the Lordships. As a result of that, English speakers were encouraged to settle in those areas. It was reinforced by the Act of Union which basically made English the official language of Wales. It meant that if you wanted to get on, you had to learn English, not Welsh. Welsh was not the language of administration or government or the legal areas; it just wasn't allowed. So Welsh speakers who were active in those areas would have to learn English. Amongst the mass of the population in most of Wales however, up until that time and for a long time afterwards, Welsh would be the first language.

If most of the linguistic traffic has been one way, however, Welsh has nonetheless left its stamp firmly on the English of this border area. The intonation pattern of Welsh with its melodic rise and fall – sometimes described somewhat disparagingly as 'sing-song' – is ubiquitous in Oswestry and not uniquely amongst families with Welsh origins. We spoke to many people who fervently professed themselves to be English, yet whose voices had that unmistakable lilt. In fact, it often results in unusual mixtures, featuring the Shropshire voiced 'r', which as we have seen resembles the West Country variety, overlaid with a songlike Welsh intonation.

To hear first hand from these hybrid speakers, Melvyn Bragg visited Pritchard's Gentlemen's Outfitters in Cross Street, to meet the proprietor, **Geraint Pritchard**:

I would define myself as a Shropshire lad really, having been born and brought up in Shropshire. But culturally, since I speak Welsh, which is of course the access into the culture, I'm culturally English and Welsh, which is the interaction that you would get of course in border areas. And as far as religion is concerned, which is a big element in border areas, I worship in Welsh, which is another factor here.

Oswestry is more English. By and large we are English, but – as occurs when a smaller language co-exists with a bigger, stronger language, the bigger language takes precedent. However, in this area, the influence of the Welsh-speaking people that live in Oswestry and come across the border into England is very, very strong, and their idioms are to be heard in English. For example, there's an intrusive sibillant 's' sound in Welsh as we know – there's no letter 'z' in Welsh – so when a Welshman speaks English, or when a Welshman who's lost his Welsh speaks English, the sibillant 's' persists. In, for example, the phrase 'Praise the Lord we're a muSSical nation'. That exists all the time, and you can identify a Welshman instantly in this area, by the intrusive 's'.

The other immediately obvious feature is the 'penultimate emphasis'. The Welsh place the stress in words on the penultimate syllable, so a Welshman speaking English would not say 'cultivator', he'd say 'cultivator' – instantly we recognise him as a Welshman.

Geraint Pritchard's experience is personal and he has a distinct lilt to his own speech. Dr Robert Penhallurick speaks with the authority of the *Survey of Anglo-Welsh Dialects*. During the 1970s, the SAWD, under the leadership of the distinguished linguist **David Parry,** carried out a careful and systematic appraisal across the Principality and in the border areas.

What we in the SAWD found in general was a lot of influence from the West Midlands of England, and a certain amount of influence from Welsh itself, coming across into the English of the area. I can give you some examples of Welsh vocabulary that we found around here:

The phrase to *cwtsh down*, meaning to squat on your haunches: the original word in Latin is *collocare*, meaning 'to lay in place', 'to lodge'. That becomes old French *coucher*, which I think means 'to hide' [modern French to sleep]. That's adopted into Middle English as *couch* – a dialectal form – and then that comes across into Welsh as *cwtsh*. And one place that it ends up is in this phrase to *cwtsh down*. So it acquires a Welsh pronunciation – *couch* becomes *cutch* – and then that *cutch* comes back in to the local English.

A similar thing has happened, I think, with the rather obscure word *mwnci* (pronounced moonkey), which meant part of a horse's harness when horses were used for ploughing. The word *mwnci* is used throughout North Wales and has been recorded in this area, again it's probably a borrowing – 'monkey' a word applied to various machines or implements – but it's the Welsh version which has been recorded in English speech, around here.

There's something of a mini-renaissance in Welsh language learning in schools in Wales. Some families in Oswestry even send their children over the border to learn Welsh and be taught other subjects in Welsh. The language is also being kept alive in public places and on signs in Oswestry itself – encouraging signs of two-way linguistic traffic.

Another good example, although it doesn't sound like a Welsh word at all, is *to keep*, used in the sense of 'to gather up and store away', as you would, say, the crockery after washing up *to keep the dishes*. This is a literal translation of an idiom in Welsh, *cadw* meaning to 'keep' or 'preserve' but which is also used in the idiomatic sense 'to put away'. It gets translated into English and the word 'keep' takes on that particular meaning, again recorded locally used as an English word – the Welsh idiom translated directly into English, and then used in English.

Dr Penhallurick points to a couple of other idioms of word-order, both of which are familiar features of Welsh English (Dylan Thomas uses them extensively, notably in *Under Milk Wood*). One is what linguists refer to as 'sentence-initial emphasis', which means putting the important bit of the sentence right at the beginning. A good example Penhallurick quotes is *singing, they were* (as opposed to 'they were singing').

The other notable example is the expression *there's...* as in *there's lovely on you*, *there's funny questions*. Again Oswestry English bears these hallmarks of the proximity of Wales and the strength of its influence.

Geraint Pritchard offers some more original examples which he has noted when chatting to customers:

These particular idioms mostly come from the agricultural world. A Welshman will never talk about laying a hedge, he will talk about *bending* a hedge, which is what we do when we bend it down. *Plygu gwrych* is the Welsh phrase. So when he speaks in English he talks about *bending* a hedge. And a Welshman would talk about *llagg gwair*, which is to *kill* hay. Well it's to 'cut' hay we say in English, which is far less descriptive. How much better to say *killing* hay. And that's an idiom which comes directly into England.

Dylan Thomas (1914–1953) recording his poems and stories for the BBC. The assonance, alliteration and internal rhyming of much of his verse – and sometimes his prose – shows the influence of the ancient bardic forms of Welsh poetry. He also liked inverting conventional word order by putting points he wished to emphasise at the beginning of a sentence, as in 'By the bridge that crosses the Dewi River, Ocky Milkman stands in the water, scooping it up in a bucket...' from *Under Milk Wood*.

Oswestry talk, though, is not totally under the influence of Welsh. From the other flank of the county come the linguistic pressures of West Midlands dialect. **Stanley Ellis**, who was one of Harold Orton's original fieldworkers on the *Survey of English Dialects*, and later Senior Lecturer at the University of Leeds, points to the way English has forced itself into the Welsh in this border territory:

There are West Midland forms, dialectal forms, that have penetrated into Welsh. The word *stondin* in Welsh, which is a 'market stall', and related to the word 'stand', is that Midlands rounding to an 'awe'-sound before a nasal, and 'n'; and you'll get *ongl* as a term for an 'angle' or a corner in quarrying. These are both Welsh words, and you'll find this rounding in the West Midlands in words like *mon* or *pon* for 'man' and 'pan'. So the dialect itself has influenced Welsh as well.

On the playing fields behind the Village Hall at Llanymynech (so borderline that the local pub has one end of the bar in England and the other in Wales), it is now too dark for the youngsters of Oswestry Youth Football team to practise. **Russell Humphries** has retired to the touchline to chat about Shropshire talk. His accent betrays no trace of Welsh influence, not a melodic intonation in earshot. But he sounds his 'r's, as a good Shropshire man, and is aware that when chatting to his mates his accent relaxes into broad Oswestrian.

I wanna, I monna, I canna, I shanna, I dunna: Shropshire slang. You just let it go when you're just casually speaking to people. So you donna say your *monna*, like, and you'll tell the lads not to do something: *donna do that!* You don't say 'I can't do that', it's *I canna do that*. 'I shouldn't do that' becomes *I shanna do that*. You know its just shortening it really. I think it's just to speed up because they're quite fast-speaking, Shropshire people, so they reckon.

Language, then, in this border region is an unspoken territory of assertion and defence, of cultural strength and identity. While Welsh embodies that yearning sense of *hiraeth* (akin to the German attachment to home described in the word *heimat*) characteristic of a cherished and embattled language and culture, the English of Oswestry is all-pervading and all-powerful. But – as we have said so many times in this book – just look at the map and note the makeup of the place names and it is clear that the linguistic highground is not entirely occupied by English. Here are the English villages of Llanymynech, Llawnt, Selatyn, Llansilin, Morda, Rhydycroesau...

Geraint Pritchard, as a Welsh speaking Englishman, is highly critical:

The pronunciation of Welsh names in Oswestry is abominable, because we English – I'm a Shropshire man, remember – we're so lazy! And there are some wonderful Welsh names in or just on the border, but the English pronunciations are disastrous. Disastrous!

These place names really are very marked. Again there are the most amazing examples of mixture. We all know the farm close by virtually on Offa's Dyke, but in England by about three miles, it's called High Fawr. Now *high* meaning 'high', and fawr meaning 'big'. Now that is a nonsense ... But it's because we're border people, we live with these things.

In 2001, Oswestry will host the *Powys Eisteddfod*, a travelling words and music festival characteristic of Welsh-speaking areas. There will be, we were assured, bilingual competitions where English learners of the Welsh language will not be at a disadvantage. But for the most part this is a quintessentially Welsh event, in spite of its taking place in an English town. Correspondingly, Oswestry Town FC is the only English club to play in the Football League of Wales. Oswestry parents in Welsh-speaking families now frequently bus their young children across the border to receive their education through the medium of the Welsh language, a provision of the education system in the Principality. Now, too, they can continue to be taught in Welsh through secondary education. And we perceived a distinct feeling that the Welsh language (thanks perhaps to Channel Four Wales television) was less embattled in these border regions than it has been in recent history. However, for all this optimism, **David Ellis**, chairman of the Oswestry branch of the National Farmers' union, sees an increasing threat:

It's difficult to see how things will progress. Very often people are educated through the medium of Welsh but then, at the end of the day, they've got to go over to England or abroad to get work, and that's where the difficulty lies, really. There are not enough jobs in Wales for the language to really get a grip on an area. And we're seeing some of the smaller communities on the border here where there's a lot of influx of English-speaking people and the communities are finding it difficult to keep the Welsh culture going. That's very sad, I think. And yet there's a tremendous amount of effort being put in by the Welsh people. It's a battle.

And it's all more difficult now. ... In general, the farming community have played a very big role in the cultural activities in their communities but with farming going downhill and units getting larger and fewer farming people in the countryside, a lot of those people have got less time on their hands to do things. It's the same in Oswestry: we're inviting the *Powys Eisteddfod* here next year and we've got a small number of Welsh-speaking people who are quite active. But it's quite a difficult task really and a lot of money to raise and finding enough people to help and most of those are the older generation. It's a struggle.

Listening to the Oswestry lads down at Llanymynech, kicking the living daylights out of their football and metaphorically out of the Welsh, you can see why.

Acknowledgements

Sincere thanks are due to everyone who has taken part in this exploration of Britain's dialects, but especially to those specialists who have shared their enthusiasm and wealth of knowledge with the Routes team throughout the series:

Stanley Ellis
Dr Clive Upton, University of Leeds
Paul Foulkes
Dominic Watt
Joan Beal, University of Newcastle
Raymond Reed
Jim Slaughter
Mike Kirkup
Dr Loreto Todd, Professor of English, University of Ulster, Coleraine
Gerry Anderson
Brian Lacey
Dr Kevin McCafferty, University of Tromsø
Sam Burnside
Richard and Jan Gendall
Nick Darke
Bert Biscoe
Linton Kwesi Johnson
Gertrude Buscher
Professor Jim Walvin, University of York
Mark Sebba, University of Lancaster
Ian Diefenthaller
Tony Thorne, King's College London
Dr Laura Wright, University of Cambridge
Dr Robert Penhallurick, University of Wales, Swansea
Professor John Wells, University College London
Dr Lynda Mugglestone, University of Oxford
Ben Elton

Thanks also to the staff and pupils of Ashington High School; Thornhill School, Derry; Penair School, Truro; and Lillian Baylis School, Brixton.

Huge gratitude to BBC colleagues on the series who have helped get the shows on the road:
Helen Boaden, Controller Radio 4, for her constant support and encouragement
Bella Bannerman, co-producer, for triumphing against the odds
Emma-Louise Williams, researcher, for her exhaustive delving and matchless casting
Christine Saunders, broadcast assistant, for putting up with all of us.